Curriculum Studies Worldwide

Series editors
William F. Pinar
Department of Curriculum and Pedagogy
University of British Columbia
Vancouver, BC, Canada

Janet L. Miller
Teachers College
New York, NY, USA

This series supports the internationalization of curriculum studies worldwide. At this historical moment, curriculum inquiry occurs within national borders. Like the founders of the International Association for the Advancement of Curriculum Studies, we do not envision a world-wide field of curriculum studies mirroring the standardization the larger phenomenon of globalization threatens. In establishing this series, our commitment is to provide support for complicated conversation within and across national and regional borders regarding the content, context, and process of education, the organizational and intellectual center of which is the curriculum.

More information about this series at
http://www.springer.com/series/14948

Fang Wang · Leslie N.K. Lo

Navigating Educational Change in China

Contemporary History and Lived Experiences

palgrave
macmillan

Fang Wang
Northeast Normal University
Changchun, China

Leslie N.K. Lo
Beijing Normal University
Beijing, China

Curriculum Studies Worldwide
ISBN 978-3-319-63614-6   ISBN 978-3-319-63615-3   (eBook)
DOI 10.1007/978-3-319-63615-3

Library of Congress Control Number: 2017948719

Cover illustration: © Melisa Hasan

Printed on acid-free paper

This Palgrave Macmillan imprint is published by Springer Nature
The registered company is Springer International Publishing AG
The registered company address is: Gewerbestrasse 11, 6330 Cham, Switzerland

This book is published under the auspices of the Teacher Studies and Development Project at the Education University of Hong Kong and Beijing Normal University.

ACKNOWLEDGEMENTS

This book is the fruit of conversation, collaboration, and reflection sustained over a period of 3 years. First conceived as a journal article, its eventual length warranted publication in book form. The authors' original intention was to narrate the lived experiences of a senior academic in the changing milieu of higher education in China but further thoughts arose on two strands of ideas that emerged from the interviews with the professor—the relationship between tradition, modernity, and postmodernity and the contrariety between indigenous Chinese values and practices and those that were imported from the West. It seemed that an observation on the professor's treatment of these ideas is essential to his intellectual history, no matter how briefly it is to be presented.

Professor William Pinar provided the idea of an intellectual history of the subject's lived experiences. He also gave critical comments on the embryonic draft of the essay and suggested a change of course on its route to publication, which shaped the narrative presented in this book. We are most grateful for this guidance.

We thank the Tin Ka Ping Foundation in Hong Kong for its generous support, which created opportunities for the authors to meet for the planning of this project.

The Center for Teacher Education Research at the Beijing Normal University facilitated a continuous dialogue between the authors through a visiting scholarship and its sustained support of the research.

Funding of the research and writing of this book come partially from the Teacher Studies and Development Project at the Education University of Hong Kong and Beijing Normal University.

Mr. John Cable has provided expert editorial guidance for this book. We are indebted to him for his timely advice and critical suggestions that have helped us make necessary improvements to the book manuscript.

We offer our special thanks to Prof. Teacher Yu for sharing his experiences and insights in delightful conversations. His readiness to enlighten is inspiring, and his trust in our constancy of purpose is deeply appreciated.

From the conceptualization of this book to the choice of its topics, we have tapped the wisdom of generations of scholars, both Chinese and Western. Colleagues and students in Changchun, Beijing, and Hong Kong have helped us to give voice to the lived experiences of the professor, from conversation and critique to voice recording and transcription. However, the faults in this book remain our own.

CONTENTS

About the Authors

Fang Wang is Associate Professor in Curriculum Studies at the Faculty of Education at Northeast Normal University in Changchun, China, where she received a doctorate degree in curriculum and teaching.

Leslie N.K. Lo is Professor at the Faculty of Education and a senior research fellow at the Center for Teacher Education Research at Beijing Normal University, China.

CHAPTER 1

Introduction

Abstract A sketch of the encounter between two academics provides the background for this book. It is observed that previous studies on Chinese education have mainly focused on the system but not the person, and that more attention should be given to the agency of individual educators who work to change the system. The present study is inspired by the emergence of a critical discourse on the lived experiences of individual educators. It attempts to elucidate the intellectual and professional pathways of one Chinese professor who has served as a scholar, teacher, and administrators in Chinese higher education. From interviews that have spanned several years, his views constitute a reflection on the complexity of educational change in China through the lens of a senior academic.

Keywords Case study · Education professor · Intellectual history Chinese higher education

THE ENCOUNTER

The dean of education sat in his office, waiting for the arrival of an important guest. The office was obviously too small for his huge book collection, and since he had moved into it, he had chosen to work at an ordinary IKEA desk hidden behind walls of books and journals. As the head of the university's largest academic unit, Teacher Yu had been appointed dean of a newly constituted faculty of education, which was

© The Author(s) 2018   1
F. Wang and L.N. K. Lo, *Navigating Educational Change in China,*
Curriculum Studies Worldwide, DOI 10.1007/978-3-319-63615-3_1

intended to consolidate the myriad functions of a growing number of units with clear affiliation to educational studies. Teacher Yu had a number of embryonic ideas for moving the faculty forward in an increasingly competitive environment of Chinese higher education. Even though these ideas were a mixture of aspirations toward enhanced branding, the scholarship of his faculty, professed beliefs in an axiological anchor for curriculum and teaching, and undefined actions targeting internationalization, he believed that they could bring the faculty to a new stage of development.

Ordinarily, Teacher Yu could talk endlessly about his ideas, for he liked to sound out others on new ideas, particularly his students. He was always nice to his students, taking them out for food, drinks and singing, and expounding with them his views on postmodernism and the future of Chinese education, but as he awaited the arrival of his guest, he was focusing expectantly on the scholarly dialogue that he hoped, with some trepidation, would emerge during his meeting with the visitor.

The visitor, William Pinar, a professor at the University of British Columbia in Canada, was an important figure in Curriculum Studies. His new approach to curriculum inquiry, the *Currere*, was well known among certain academic pockets in China. Teacher Yu appreciated Pinar's book, *Understanding Curriculum*, and considered it a major theoretical source for his study of postmodernism. He later confided to the visitor that he had read the voluminous monograph thrice. The meeting with Pinar was the highlight of the day for Teacher Yu, for it provided a pleasant diversion from the mundane duties of a dean.

When Pinar was escorted into the dean's office, Teacher Yu was burying himself in work, teapot within reach but the flowers and fruits that were the standard paraphernalia for the reception of foreign guests were noticeable by their absence. Instead of the drawn-out ceremonial greetings that were a part of the protocol, Teacher Yu took Pinar for a tour of his book collection. The books on his shelves were a collection of philosophical, educational, and historical books, some various editions of the same titles, and tomes, some recondite, by certain historical figures in the disciplines that formed his "academic foundation." Teacher Yu wanted to share the excitement of having owned certain "treasures" in his book collection with Pinar. He climbed the ladder-stool a few times to retrieve books in Chinese or English to show the visitor—a rare edition of the *Analect* here and the inaugural lecture of a prominent scholar there. Before long, the host and the visitor realized that they shared ample common interest in the thoughts of Foucault, Derrida, Dewey, Locke, Whitehead, Kant, and Weber, to name but few. It appeared that what had been merely a courtesy visit had become an occasion for true scholarly bonding.

Before his departure from China, Pinar remarked to his guide, a young teacher in his host's faculty, that "it would be interesting to learn about Yu's intellectual history." At the time, he was actively involved in a project that examined the development of Curriculum Studies in various parts of the world through the study of the intellectual histories of individual scholars. His meeting with Teacher Yu had naturally led him to focus his lens on the intellectual development of a scholar who was a fellow traveler on a parallel path of scholarship.

Subsequently, the young teacher talked to dean Yu about being interviewed for the project. She said it would be a study of his intellectual history, approached from multiple perspectives that would include his personal academic influences. Dean Yu agreed and it was decided to focus the study on his ideas, education, and work. The interviews continued over the course of two years, and this book is a record of those interviews. Soon after the first interview, it was learned that Teacher Yu would take up yet another change of appointment, becoming the principal of one of the university's affiliated primary schools.

∗∗∗∗∗∗∗∗∗∗∗∗∗∗

Observers of Chinese education today tend to see it as one of the driving forces behind China's rapid rise as a world power. The transformation of Chinese education from near-dormancy to vibrant revival has captured the interest of educators around the world. The expansion of its education system has made learning available to millions of children in some of the poorest regions in the country. A dramatic increase in university enrollment, further augmented by widespread participation in distance learning, has elevated the quality of China's workforce to a new height. The recent outstanding performance of Shanghai students in international assessments of academic achievement may be taken as evidence of the country's educational success.

Its impressive achievements notwithstanding, Chinese education has also displayed gross disparities among geographic regions and various types of schools and higher institutions. Implementation of educational and curricular reforms has yielded uneven results, favoring schools in the more affluent localities. Schooling is still examination-oriented, and university students spend too much time on attending lectures rather than on activities that can enrich their college experiences. As the world learns to appreciate the strengths and limitations of Chinese education through reports, studies, and visits, more questions have surfaced regarding the future direction of its educational institutions, the aspirations of its students and teachers, and the deeper meaning of China's educational development.

Our understanding of Chinese education has been informed by personal experiences, formal study in academic courses, observations in field research, and a steady flow of observations embedded in the literature in the field. A continuous survey of literature has given the authors the impression that, until recently, noteworthy studies on the educational development in China have mainly focused on the education system or a sector of the system rather than on its stakeholders, such as teachers and students. This tendency is especially discernible in early publications that purport to be "value-neutral" studies, which delineate the broad economic and political forces that have shaped the modernization of education in China.[1]

In the research for this book, we dug deeper into the literature and found that there was a conspicuous absence of "the person" in English language publications on Chinese education. There are a few early studies on Chinese educators, but they are generally considered as studies of Chinese intellectuals, a study of a social group that had left a strong imprint on the country's development.[2] Studies on Chinese educators, then, are mostly portrayals of prominent public intellectuals serving in the capacity of educators.[3] The focus of these studies is mainly on their place in the system and their role in bringing about systemic changes. Their life and work are posited in the broad context of general societal development, not in educational settings. Their trials and tribulations and their individual struggles as educators are masked by the system which evolved under their stewardship. Such an absence fails to reflect the flavor or color, or emphasize the capacity of education as a social institution by not giving due consideration to the agency of individual educators who work to change the system.

A critical discourse on the agency of individual educators is important because they constitute a major constituency in the education system. Their journeys crisscross the educational landscape shaping its contours of thought and practice. Along the pathways of their life and work, educational insights can be gained from the personal experiences of these educators. The ways that individual educators frame and make sense of their worlds and life-changing events represent not only their own ideas and thinking but also reflect the intellectual currents of their times.

GUIDING LITERATURE

Three studies have mainly inspired the writing of this book. Their approaches to studying Chinese educators mark a noteworthy departure from the mainstream literature. Rather than treating the contribution of the person to the system as their principal concern, these studies situate individual educators as persons at the center of their exploration. The examination of the ideas, values, and identity in relation to the personal histories of individual Chinese educators affords an intimate portrayal of persons responding to shifting situations in their lives. Some of these educators are scholar-teachers of an older generation who have anchored the development of educational studies in China. Others are educators who have crossed national and cultural borders to work in different educational settings. Still, others are experts in Curriculum Studies who have contributed to the establishment of the field in China.

In her book, *Portraits of Influential Chinese Educators*, published in Hayhoe 2007, Ruth Hayhoe adopts a "narrative approach" to the study of eleven prominent scholars in contemporary Chinese education. The work of these influential educators is discussed in terms of their contribution to various sub-fields of educational studies, such as comparative education, theory of learning, higher education, philosophy of education, and moral education. Their life experiences as members of families, institutions, communities, and nation are examined along with an exposition of their core values and educational views. The study gives voice to a group of scholar-teachers that is influential in educational studies in China but has had only limited exposure in Western literature. In the process of creating portraits of these educators with findings from interviews and reading, the author found a common theme threading through the life stories of the educators. It was the Confucian heritage—the writing and teaching of Confucius that upheld the sense of self-worth and self-respect of the individual—that had served as an essential foundation for the lives and thoughts of the educators. As persons who suffered personal attacks during the Cultural Revolution when Confucianism also came under severe criticism, these educators had embraced it in their lives and work. Through education, they had persevered in keeping alive a key aspect of their cultural heritage with a clear sense of intellectual purpose.

Another source of inspiration for this study is Hongyu Wang's book, *Nonviolence and Education: Cross-cultural pathways* (2014), which is a study of the cross-cultural pathways of four university professors. It explores the lived experiences of two Chinese and two American professors at the intersection of the individual, society and history, and weaving the autobiographical and the global. Wang places autobiographical reflection at the center of her inquiry in an attempt to relate the meaning of the subjects' work to their personal awareness. It is the individual's "engagement in his or her unique pathway that is the center of attention," she claims, "not intergroup relationship." To her, the site of education "is ultimately individual personhood" (p. xii). Individual pathways of shifts and situations are thus explored through interviews with the four academics who remain anonymous. Details of the interviews precede reflections by Wang, who draws on Chinese and American intellectual traditions. With extensive reference made to the works on Daoism, Buddhism, and American nonviolent activism, the author's commitment to formulating a vision of nonviolence in Curriculum Studies is clearly discernible.

The third source of inspiration for this study is William Pinar's book, *Curriculum Studies in China: Intellectual histories, present circumstances* (2014). In his study, Pinar assembles essays by eight Chinese scholars which narrate their intellectual histories in relation to the present circumstances of Curriculum Studies in China. The scholars' journeys are situated in history, culture, international developments, and educational contexts. The stories of the Chinese scholars are given depth by Pinar's interviews with them, by the essays that they composed, and by the "protracted exchanges" of views that the author conducted with three experts in order to provide an informed and assessable range of curricula in China in both historical and current contexts. The goal of these efforts is to illuminate "the acumen, sensitivity, and insight" of the perspective of the Chinese scholars (Pinar 2014, p. 2). In the spirit of "Currere"—a methodological concept developed by Pinar to elucidate educational experiences through autobiographical reflection (Pinar 1975)—the book mines the intellectual history and present commitments of each scholar and attempts to demonstrate the unique ways in which these individuals understood and made sense of their own circumstances within the larger context curriculum development in China. Pinar's book serves to inspire the present study as a methodological compass that points to the possibility of unearthing authentic educational concerns through reflections on personal history. It also exemplifies a linkage that can be built between the private passion of the educators and the larger cultural and historical context of their past.

The books by Hayhoe, Wang, and Pinar have laid the groundwork for a new approach to the study of Chinese educators. The use of life histories, grounded in the personal experiences of the participating educators, provides an alternative pathway of intellectual exploration that can serve as an invigorating parallel to the conventional mode of investigation. All three studies point to the critical dimensions of time and space in the shifting circumstances of the educators' lives. Pinar's study of the curriculum scholars yields an understanding of the meaning of their intellectual pursuits, which are seen as "a shifting and situated series" that "reconstructs private passion into public service" (Pinar 2014, p. 2). In their self-reflective essays, the eight scholars offer insights into how they changed the curriculum in China and were in turn changed by its reconstruction. The lived experiences of the curriculum experts, as depicted in their essays, are captured by critical events that occurred in different junctures of their individual journeys of becoming—finding one's direction and situation, studying abroad, changing specializations, or simply holding to one's beliefs and purposes. At the core of their intellectual development is a communion with the nation's history and culture that is present in their personal stories. The same affinity to history and culture is discernible in the life histories of the influential Chinese educators that Hayhoe narrates. Whereas these educators lived and worked in unique institutional contexts, they shared a common adherence to the Confucian way of being scholar-teachers who cultivated themselves determinedly in order to shoulder social responsibilities. In telling the stories of her educators, Hayhoe was aware of the issues that surrounded the multiple layers of time in her narration "...time past, in memory, time present, in attention, and time future, in expectation" (Hayhoe 2004: 330). Similarly, the stories of Wang's four professors illuminate the essentiality of life history and cultural space in the study of educators who crossed national and cultural borders to engage with others in educational settings that are different from their own. By situating the four professors at the intersection of the individual, society, and history, Wang explores how life chances and situated personhood affect cross-cultural engagements.

Taken together, the above studies illustrate the essentiality of understanding human existence in the exploration of educational phenomena, which envelops the person in the interplay of history, culture, and community. Through the study of the lived experiences of the person, it is possible to unearth a deeper understanding of the larger educational context in which he or she lives.

PURPOSE OF THE BOOK

The purpose of this book is to elucidate the intellectual and professional pathways of one Chinese professor who has made his mark as a scholar, teacher, and administrator in China's higher education. It is a reflection on the complexity of educational change in China through the lens of a senior academic. From his experience as an observer of political upheavals, being a student of the philosophy of education, thought worker for undergraduates, university teacher and administrator, and the principal of an elite urban primary school, we revisit certain landmarks in his intellectual journey and examine the impact of change on Chinese education at important historic junctures. As the lived experience of this professor demonstrates, the contemporary history of Chinese education, as embedded in the personal accounts of the individual, is a series of memories of change and uncertainty. However, it is in the fluid context of change that the agency of the individual can best be illuminated.

In this narrative, the professor is situated at the intersection of history, culture, society, and the individual where the search for personal identity becomes a lifelong project. Like other educators of his time, he has lived and worked in an institutional context that struggles to strike a balance between tradition and modernity, and to translate foreign (mostly Western) ideas into blueprints for indigenous practices. It is in such a fluid institutional context that the agency of the individual becomes more pronounced. The political imperative that Chinese education should retain its own cultural and national character while striving to modernize has made the challenge more complex for the professor who has occupied several key positions at his university. His story is about making transitions between the different worlds of the Chinese academe while trying to find an intellectual and professional anchor.

METHODS OF INQUIRY AND EMERGING THEMES

The present study is based on information collected from five formal interviews with the professor and studies of his academic essays.

The five interviews, conducted in Chinese by the first author, took place over the course of several years. The first interview took place in 2009, preceding the planning of this book. The ensuing interviews took place during 2014–2016. Each interview lasted for about two hours. Information collected from the interviews was supplemented and clarified by more informal conversations and correspondence with the professor. Transcripts of interviews were shared with the professor for verification of accuracy. Initially, in order to construct a preliminary framework for the interviews with the professor, we adopted the questions that Pinar used in his interviews with the Chinese curriculum experts (Pinar 2014) as our guide. These questions touch upon myriad aspects of the intellectual histories of his participating scholars—from the genesis of their present intellectual pursuits to the imagined "next steps" for scholarly and professional advancement—with the intention of situating their endeavors in the larger institutional and societal contexts. The Pinar questions were used in the early interviews, but, as the conversations with the professor led to fresh topics of interest, the list of questions underwent a metamorphosis as new outlooks, with concerns that were directly related to his experiences, emerged.

The academic essays that have been selected for research purpose are among the professor's most noteworthy publications and have direct relevance to the topics of discussion. Among the topics are his views on the place of modernity and postmodernity in Chinese education and on the indigenization of education in an age of globalization. As all of his publications are written in Chinese, extracted passages in his written essays are translated for use in this book. Additionally, the first author has kept a research journal that records personal observations and feelings throughout the research process. This journal has proved to be a useful resource for reflection, especially when the injection of more contextual information in the text was found necessary.

The interviews aim to situate the professor in multiple layers of time and space. For that, the intellectual history of the professor is revealed by a continuous dialogue on his lived experiences. Our conversations were sustained by a mode of interviewing that allowed him to digress, with questions injected mainly for clarification or in pursuit of fresh topics. As the interviews progressed, several interrelated issues have emerged. For the purpose of this study, we have translated them into the following research questions that have guided the writing of this book: (1) Under what historical, social, and educational circumstances did the professor choose his pursuits that have led to diverse academic and professional experiences? (2) For the development of Chinese education and society, how does he reconcile the differences between tradition and modernity, and the tensions between the foreign and the indigenous? (3) How does he make sense of the educational and societal changes that have shaped the conditions of his work and identity?

Our attempt to address the above research questions has led to a series of themes that form the basis of inquiry for each of the book's chapters. These themes are as follows: (1) memories and images of important events and significant others in the professor's life; (2) his views on tradition, modernity, and postmodernity; (3) his understanding of the tensions arising from the interaction between the indigenous and the foreign; and (4) his search for identity in the varied terrain of educational change.

THE CHOICE OF TEACHER YU

Our choice of "Teacher Yu, the professor" is based on the uniqueness of his pursuits, on the one hand, and the commonalities that he shares with his compatriot educators, on the other hand. By placing his thoughts, feelings, and actions at the center of our inquiry, we hope to offer a fresh look at the development of contemporary Chinese education through the lens of human agency. Teacher Yu is an educator who has played different roles in a normal university which has remained his sole employer since he left college. An examination of how he has made the transition between the site of scholarship and the site of administrative work, and how he has made sense of his world will carry the narrative beyond the confines of systemic goals and strategies (Werts and Brewer 2015: 207).

In a way, the journey of Teacher Yu is similar to many of his contemporaries as it has been shaped by sociopolitical forces of history and personal choices he has made. He is an academic in his early fifties who chose to work for his *alma mater*, a common practice for many university teachers of his time. Like many academics in his age group, he has never gone abroad to study. He gained experience working as a student counselor in the university without earning a formal master's degree and pursued his doctoral study part-time at the same university. His career as a university teacher seems to have followed the usual path of ascension, from lectureship to full professorship. However, it is the various transitions among political, academic, and administrative positions that distinguish him from his peers with purely academic interests. From the multiple positions that he has held, it appears that he has earned the trust of university leaders who are always looking for capable academics to help them run their institution.[4]

The uniqueness of Teacher Yu's journey actually rests with his eventual immersion in school education when he was appointed as the principal of an elite primary school that is affiliated with the university. The appointment opens up new opportunities that are available to very few university teachers in educational studies. As a professor of philosophy of education, his work at the primary school distinguishes him as a scholar-practitioner who has been awarded an opportunity that allows him to practice what he preaches. As a professional educator, his direct involvement in school education allows his work to be extended to other parts of the education system, from university to school. The ways in which he interprets and executes numerous and varied policies, rules and regulations, affect the growth of students of all capacities. His views on education, when applied to different educational settings, represent the ways that he, as an educator and teacher, makes sense of the educational reality in certain historical contexts. His choice of actions reflects his discernment of the reality in education at the time, as well as his values and ideas about the appropriateness of his decisions. Teacher Yu is a reflexive practitioner who holds the interests of his students and the institution paramount, and he has been ambivalent about revealing his identity and affiliation. We have therefore decided to use the anonym "Teacher Yu," a name that all his students use when addressing him, in this book.

NOTES

1. Most of the early publications on Chinese education under Communism were collections of translated documents from Chinese sources which were framed according to policy-related topics and interpreted with lengthy introductions. For example, see, Fraser (1965), Seybolt (1973), Chen (1974), Hu (1974), Hu and Seifman (1976). The study of Chinese education became more specialized, and the convergence of the humanities and social science disciplines provided a more analytic structure of inquiry for the field. See, for instance, Nee (1969), Wu and Sheeks (1970), Ridley et al. (1971), White (1981), Shirk (1982), Unger (1982). Toward the turn of the century, works on numerous topics in modern and contemporary Chinese education were published, from its dealing with tradition and modernity (Cleverley 1991) to orientations of educational reform

(Pepper 1996), and from higher education (Hayhoe 1996; Yang 2002) to the privatization of schooling (Lin 1999). With increased opportunities in the field of research and the availability of research data, Chinese education now affords comparison with education in other societies (Tobin et al. 1991, 2009) or reflection as a possible model for borrowing by Western societies (Zhao 2014).

2. Early studies on Chinese intellectuals reflect a concerted effort on the part of Western scholars to identify them as a driving force behind the country's modernization endeavor and to explain their roles in related projects (for example, Teng and Fairbank 1979; Spence 1981). Initially, studies on Chinese intellectuals have focused on their roles as thinkers who attempted to enlighten their peers (Schwartz 1964); as reformers who sought to alter the country's course of development (Levenson 1953; Levenson 1969; Ayers 1971); and as revolutionaries who attempted to replace the old social order with a drastically different one (Snow 1938; Meisner 1967). Under different political regimes, the roles that individual intellectuals chose to play reflected their own ideological persuasions, from being loyal supporters of the powers that be to being active dissenters of state policies (Goldman 1981). Others have chosen to remain critical observers of the affairs of the state and society (for example, Lin 1935; Pollard 2003; Davies 2013). As the career paths of Chinese intellectuals have become more diverse since the birth of a market economy, some of them have opted to engage in entrepreneurship (Liu 2001) and kept a safe distance from the center of political power. The expansion of career choices toward the end of the twentieth century opened up new opportunities for intellectuals but has also caused a decline in their influence in China's political affairs (Goldman and Lee 2002; Hao 2003).

3. For example, the intellectual biography of Cai Yuanpei, who was a minister of education in the Republican government and later became the chancellor of Peking University, is designed to illustrate the tensions between Western and Confucian values and attitudes and to explain the failure of an attempt to transplant Western institutions in the Chinese society (Duiker 1977). Likewise, the biographical studies on James Yen (Hayford 1990), an international renowned reformer of rural education, and Liang Shuming (Alitto 1979), a Confucian philosopher who also initiated a large-scale mass education project for the rural masses, have placed emphasis on their roles as social reformers and how their work impacted on the life of the masses. In this vein, Tao Xingzhi, who is the most revered educator in modern Chinese history, has received less attention in Western literature, either as a reformer or an educator (for example, Brown 1990).

4. In China's higher institutions today, the scarcity of administratively capable senior academics is a consequence of a ten-year "talent gap" that is

attributed to the closure of schools and universities during the days of the Great Proletariat Cultural Revolution (1966–1976). The significant disruption of supply of "fresh blood" into academia has made the availability of younger talents, now in their late forties and early fifties, seem greater than previously. The appointment of these academics into senior academic and administrative positions through early promotion at around the turn of the century was a common phenomenon in Chinese higher education.

REFERENCES

Alitto, G. S. (1979). *The last Confucian: Liang Shu-ming and the Chinese dilemma of modernity.* Berkeley, CA: University of California Press.

Ayers, W. (1971). *Chang Chih-tung and educational reform in China.* Cambridge, MA: Harvard University Press.

Brown, H. O. (1990). Tao Xingzhi: Progressive educator in Republic of China. *Biography, 13*(1), 21–42. doi:10.1353/bio.2010.0419.

Chen, T. H. E. (1974). *The Maoist educational revolution.* New York: Praeger.

Cleverley, J. F. (1991). *The schooling of China: Tradition and modernity in Chinese education* (2nd ed.). North Sydney, NSW: Allen & Unwin.

Davies, G. (2013). *Lu Xun's revolution: Writings in a time of violence.* Cambridge, MA: Harvard University Press.

Duiker, W. J. (1977). *Tsai Yuan-pei: Educator of Modern China.* University Park, PA: Pennsylvania State University Press.

Fraser, S. (Ed.). (1965). *Chinese Communist education: Records of the first decade.* Nashville, TN: Vanderbilt University Press.

Goldman, M. (1981). *China's intellectuals: Advice and dissent.* Cambridge, MA: Harvard University Press.

Goldman, M., & Lee, L. O. F. (Eds.). (2002). *An intellectual history of Modern China.* New York: Cambridge University Press.

Hao, Z.D. (2003). *Intellectuals at a crossroad: The changing politics of China's knowledge workers.* Albany, NY: State University of New York Press.

Hayford, C. W. (1990). *To the people: James Yen and village China.* New York: Columbia University Press.

Hayhoe, R. (1996). *China's universities, 1895–1995: A century of cultural conflict.* New York: Routledge.

Hayhoe, R. (2004). Ten lives in mine: Creating portraits of influential Chinese educators. *International Journal of Education Research, 41*(4–5), 324–338. doi:10.1016/j.ijer.2005.08.004.

Hayhoe, R. (2007). *Portraits of influential Chinese educators.* Dordrecht: Springer.

Hu, C. T. (Ed.). (1974). *Chinese education under Communism.* New York: Teachers College Press.

Hu, S. M., & Seifman, E. (Eds.). (1976). *Toward a new world outlook: A documentary history of education in the People's Republic of China*. New York: AMS Press.

Levenson, J. R. (1953). *Liang Ch'i-Ch'ao and the mind of Modern China*. Cambridge, MA: Harvard University Press.

Levenson, J. R. (1969). *Confucian China and its modern fate: A trilogy*. Berkeley, CA: University of California Press.

Lin, Y.T. (1935). *My country and my people*. New York: Reynal & Hitchcock, Inc. (A John Day Book).

Lin, J. (1999). *Social transformation and private education in China*. New York: Praeger.

Liu, X. W. (2001). *Jumping into the seas: From academics to entrepreneurs in South China*. New York: Rowman & Littlefield.

Meisner, M. (1967). *Li Ta-chao and the origins of Chinese Marxism*. Cambridge, MA: Harvard University Press.

Nee, V., & Layman, D. (1969). *Cultural revolution at Peking University*. New York: Monthly Review Press.

Pepper, S. (1996). *Radicalism and education reform in 20th century China*. New York: Cambridge University Press.

Pinar, W. F. (1975). *The method of "Currere"*. Paper presented at the annual meeting of the American Educational Research Association in 1975, Washington, DC. Cited in ERIC: ED104766.

Pinar, W. F. (2014). *Curriculum Studies in China: Intellectual histories, present circumstances*. New York: Palgrave Macmillan.

Pollard, D. P. (2003). *The true story of Lu Xun*. Hong Kong: Chinese University Press.

Ridley, C. P., Doolin, D., & Godwin, P. (1971). *The making of a model citizen in Communist China*. Stanford, CA: Hoover Institution Press.

Schwartz, B. (1964). *In search of wealth and power: Yen Fu and the West*. Cambridge, MA: Harvard University Press.

Seybolt, P. J. (Ed.). (1973). *Revolutionary education in China: Documents and commentary*. White Plains, NY: M.E. Sharpe.

Shirk, S. (1982). *Competitive comrades: Career incentives and student strategies in China*. Berkeley, CA: University of California Press.

Snow, E. (1938). *Red star over China*. New York: Random House.

Spence, J. D. (1981). *The Gate of Heavenly Peace: The Chinese and their revolution, 1895–1980*. New York: Viking Press.

Teng, S. Y., & Fairbank, J. K. (1979). *China's response to the west: A documentary survey, 1939–1923*. Cambridge, MA: Harvard University Press.

Tobin, J. J., Wu, D. Y. H., & Davidson, D. (1991). *Preschool in three cultures, Japan, China and the United States*. New Haven, CT: Yale University Press.

Tobin, J. J., Yeh, H., & Karasawa, M. (2009). *Preschool in three cultures revisited.* Chicago: University of Chicago Press.

Unger, J. (1982). *Education under Mao: Class and competition in Canton schools, 1960–1980.* New York: Columbia University Press.

Wang, H. Y. (2014). *Nonviolence and education: Cross-cultural pathways.* New York: Routledge.

Werts, A. B., & Brewer, C. A. (2015). Reframing the study of policy implementation: Lived experience as politics. *Educational Policy, 29*(1), 206–229.

White, G. (1981). *Party and professionals: The political role of teachers in contemporary China.* Armonk, NY: M.E. Sharpe.

Wu, Y. L., & Sheeks, R. B. (1970). *The organization and support of scientific research and development in Mainland China.* New York: Praeger for the National Science Foundation.

Yang, R. (2002). *Third delight: The internationalization of higher education in China.* New York: Routledge.

Zhao, Y. (2014). *Who's afraid of the big bad dragon: Why China has the best (and worst) education system in the world.* San Francisco: Jossey-Bass.

CHAPTER 2

Memories and Imageries

Abstract Early life's lessons in altruism, perseverance, and the influence of societal forces on a person's life combined to mold the professor's values and outlook. The choice of staying in the academe as a political worker after graduation afforded a decade of steady employment, but it also bred self-doubt and an identity crisis involving the question of "What am I?" The decision to pursue an academic career brought him into the field of educational philosophy. The professor enjoyed teaching and research, as well as the new status of a legitimate academic. New appointments enabled his ascension in the university's administration, but a growing awareness of the chasm between ideas and practice in the field of education led him to ask: "What am I doing?"

Keywords Life history · Political worker in Chinese University
Career mobility · Identity problems

Teacher Yu was admitted to the university in the early 1980s after the Cultural Revolution (1966–1976). It was the time when China's universities were just reopening after a decade of dormancy. Tens of thousands of people, trapped in the bottleneck of repression and despair, competed for scarce university places and hoped "to see the sky and sun again" through studying for the university entrance examinations.

Teacher Yu was good at studying and he loved "reading books, especially philosophical books" (Interview 2, 2014: 2). His application for

© The Author(s) 2018   17
F. Wang and L.N.K. Lo, *Navigating Educational Change in China*,
Curriculum Studies Worldwide, DOI 10.1007/978-3-319-63615-3_2

university admission was processed through a centralized admission system and he chose the department of philosophy at a comprehensive university as his first choice and the department of education at a normal university as his second choice.[1] He missed his out on his first choice "by a narrow margin" and settled for educational studies at the university where, without realizing it at the time, he would study, work, and build a long career (Ibid.: 1). It was his first acquaintance with educational studies. He would get his chance of pursuing formal study in philosophy later, at the doctoral level, by using education as a springboard for his inquiry into postmodernism.

Teacher Yu's predilection for philosophy, a discipline which requires a higher level of abstract thinking, lodged in still reflection, can be attributed to his disposition to focus on certain tasks that capture his attention. "When I was a little boy," he confides, "I liked to make tanks out of mud. Sometimes I could make a hundred tanks in one afternoon. I was obsessed with it. I just kept making them. I would make thousands of them in a summer even though it was tiring" (Interview 2, 2014: 2). He was a quiet boy who "often played by [himself] and was interested in abstract and difficult to understand topics" (Interview 3, 2014: 5). Even at an early age, he showed he was attracted to the abstract, to reading, and became engrossed in matters of this interest. He attributes his eventual pursuit of the study of philosophy and education to a kind of perseverance that he demonstrated in his childhood:

> I have a rather stubborn personality, and I can sit still. Studying philosophy, especially rational thinking, is something that is not very affective. If one doesn't have the required perseverance, one can't understand the readings; if one can't sit still, one can't think very thoroughly. Philosophy requires us to contemplate, not just musing, for musing is not necessarily contemplation. (Interview 2, 2014: 5)

Teacher Yu is philosophical about the people and events that are important to his life and work. He looks at fate in a determinedly secular way by linking the course of a person's life to the circumstances of the times. "In reality a person's destiny is intimately connected to the nation's destiny" (Interview 5, 2016: 2), he argues, "No one can transcend history" (Interview 2, 2014: 9). This tenet offers ready explanations for critical events that changed his life—from his choice of work to his views on academic freedom—and the lives of his significant others. From the memories and images that he retains and shares, some of these circumstances seem almost predetermined.

MEMORIES OF FAMILY AND CHILDHOOD IMAGES

Teacher Yu's family was spared of the repression of several political upheavals that have left a deep scar on the community. This refuge of peace was built on class affiliation that came as a result of the job choice of his parents and the misfortune suffered by his ancestors.

He was born into a "middle-class" family, which, by the living standard of China in the 1960s, meant that its members were free from hunger and had the bare means of existence. His father "studied machinery processing at the Jilin Industrial university" and "worked there as a mechanic after graduation" (Interview 5, 2016: 1). He was a fine artisan and, with his dexterous hands, assembled a variety of household appliances for the family, "including the heater and hot-pot," "repaired the bicycle that we used," and even "crafted from scratch a full set of tiles for the *Mahjong* game"[2] (Ibid.):

> I remember it was in the 1970s. People played *Mahjong* in their homes then. The *Mahjong* set in our home was made by my father. He cut the plastic to the size of a *Mahjong* tile, and then pressed the necessary patterns down on the plastic. It required a lot of skill. Then he used different kinds of sandpaper to smooth the tiles. They were exactly like the ones that were sold in the stores, including the characters that were carved on the tiles. (Ibid.)

According to Teacher Yu, his father was an upright, self-sufficient, and willful person who would not ask people for favors. He seldom mingled sociably with others. "Actually I don't like to socialize with people that much either," Teacher Yu confides, suggesting a comparison, "I like to do things by myself" (Ibid.). His father's disposition, however, had caused him to leave his position at the university for a factory job, which, as he found out later, offered a much less generous retirement package. "He didn't get along with his superiors. He was too headstrong and insubordinate," Teacher Yu says.

His father left the university to work in the factory in the early 1970s. The transfer, which took place during the Cultural Revolution, was urged by Teacher Yu's grandmother who worried for her son's safety.

She beseeched her son to leave the university. Teacher Yu recalls: "My grandmother was very worried. She said, 'you've got to leave the university as quickly as possible. Go and work in the factory!' It was a time when the proletariat was considered the leader of everyone. And the university was a place of quarrels and scandals" (Ibid.:1–2). The factory afforded his father a clear class identity as a worker. At the time, being an employee of a higher education institution afforded little status and security. It had become a workplace where its leaders, university administrators, and professors could be branded as "class enemies" and suffer humiliation and even physical abuse at the political struggle rallies that were frequently organized at the time. The job transfer had helped to shelter the family from political repression.

Another factor in the favorable classification of the class identity of Teacher Yu's family can be traced back to a change of family fortune that stemmed from his maternal grandfather who had been a rich peasant with a gambling habit. In an ironic twist of fate, the grandfather lost the family fortune in a *Mahjong* game before the Communists came to power. Consequently, when the new regime began dividing the populace into different categories by class distinction, the family "had the good fortune" to be classified as poor peasants. By categorization, poor peasants belonged to the oppressed class that was considered favorably by the new political regime and because of this, the family was spared the political hardship that befell so many families in subsequent political campaigns. They were safe.

Because of her new class identity, Teacher Yu's mother was spared the kind of political repression that a daughter in the "well-to-do family of a rich peasant" would have suffered. Teacher Yu describes her as a kindly woman who has played the role of a traditional homemaker, "making those padded shoes and clothing that I wore when I was young" (Interview 5, 2016: 1). He speaks fondly of his mother whenever she is mentioned during the interviews: "She worked as a primary school teacher in the village for over a decade, and then moved to the city when I was two years old…. She was more sociable and had more friends [than my father]" (Ibid.).

Because of these circumstances of history, members of Teacher Yu's family were basically bystanders that merely observed the political upheavals of the Cultural Revolution. From his memories, "sitting on my father's shoulders and watching a parade of militiamen carrying machine guns seemed exciting and joyful" (Ibid.: 2). However, the scenes from a mass political struggle rally where a prominent university official was denounced and humiliated in public by an endless stream of class hatred bile and contemptuous insults had left a strong imprint on his young mind:

> It was a violent and perilous time.... I remember that it involved the deputy director of the revolutionary committee [of the university]. He was a soldier in the 359 Brigade of the old Eighth Army. His son was a classmate of mine in primary school. He was donning a white dunce cap with characters written on it about him being some kind of anti-revolutionary. He carried a large placard on his chest. The venue [for the political struggle rally] was a small auditorium in the university. It was a building constructed during the 'Puppet Manchukuo regime'[3] and it used to be a part of the university.[4] The crowd was huge. And all the shouting! I can still remember those scenes vividly. (Ibid.: 1)

It was Teacher Yu's paternal grandmother who took him to the rally. She also took him to a memorial gathering for students who were killed during the armed confrontations on the university campus (Interview 2, 2014: 10). His grandmother lived with the family and was the major caregiver in his early years. "Because both of my parents had to work, I spent less time with them than with my grandmother. There wasn't a lot of homework in those days, so I spent most of my time with her." Teacher Yu talks about his grandmother affectionately and admiringly— from the delicious buns, dumplings, and noodles that she made to the fact that "she got up at four o'clock everyday to prepare breakfast for my father who had to go to work very early in the morning" (Interview 5, 2016: 2). She was a small woman with bound feet. She could neither read nor write, and, until the government started to implement the nationwide household registration, "she had no name" (Ibid.: 1). She was happy that she was given a name, Yu-Yang Shi, which literally means "Woman Yang married into the household of Yu." Indeed, she had played a subservient role in her marriage to a grumpy husband (Ibid.).

One thing that Teacher Yu's grandmother had taught him by example was to have compassion for others. "Her amiability and kindheartedness have deeply affected me," Teacher Yu recalls, "She was always ready to help neighbors in need, sometimes even to a point that she might have neglected her own family" (Ibid.: 2). "I've heard my mother complained about this. Sometimes she would see snow in my shoes after I played outside, and my grandmother wasn't paying attention because she was busy taking care of the neighbor's children. That made my mother unhappy" (Ibid.). This kind of altruism would continue throughout her life, as "she was always volunteering for all kinds of community service" (Ibid.: 1). Then, his grandmother passed away, after suffering years of ill health, "six months before [he took] the university entrance examination" (Ibid.).

In retrospect, Teacher Yu's grandparents shared a certain penchant for altruistic behavior toward the needy. Since his childhood, Teacher Yu had been told that his paternal grandfather was also a man of compassion, despite his bad temper:

> He was a skillful carpenter who was forthright and generous toward others. He had provided well for the family. At the time, a carpenter could earn up to a hundred catties of flour per month. Whenever there was flour left over in the family, he would give it to his friends. My father and grandmother talked about how he made money but had remained frugal. What he had, he lent it to friends. My father said that I'm like him, treating people generously and hoping my friends could have what I had.... But I never met my grandfather. He passed away five years before I was born. (Ibid.)

For Teacher Yu, his ancestors had not only set examples of altruism and charity but had also demonstrated how the human agency could foster meaning for their lives. He believes that their lives were intimately linked to history. Their thinking and behaviors reflected the norms and mores of the times. The forces of history have created for their lives an abundance of constraints and limitations, but with perseverance and a bit of good fortune, their actions could still make a difference for themselves and others.

The cases of Teacher Yu's ancestors show how a reversal of fortune could change a person's future, for better or for worse. But in the case of his beloved cousin, Dongming, the individual seems powerless to defy the currents of history that undermined the life chances of a whole generation of young people. Dongming was an artistic person of many talents. He could produce the finest drawings, play the *Erhu* (a two-stringed musical instrument), sing Peking opera, make furniture, and assemble a radio, the "Ruby Radio," which was the finest device of the era (Ibid.: 2). He was the son of Teacher Yu's paternal aunt and was fifteen years older, but he seemed willing to spend time playing with his younger cousin whenever he visited the family. During one of these visits, Teacher Yu recalls, "I suddenly got very homesick in the middle of the night. My aunt didn't know what to do as our families lived ten miles apart. It was my cousin who took me home by riding the bicycle all the way. If I had to walk home, it would be impossible. My cousin took me home" (Ibid.).

Like so many young people of his time, Dongming joined the mass of young "intellectual youths" (*zhishi qingnian*) that were dispatched by the party-state to "learn from the poor peasants" in the countryside. It was in the year 1968, and Dongming had just graduated from high school. He was supposed to spend years in the rural areas, awaiting a change of state policies to bring him back home in the city. He did not have to wait too long though. In the following year, the death of his father, who had worked at the "workers cultural palace" in the state capital of Changchun all his life, had allowed him to return to work in the city (Ibid.). At the time, the party-state had full control of the citizens' job assignment and their rights of residence. In a sense, Dongming actually "inherited" the position that was vacated by his late father. The "workers cultural palace"—a major venue for recreational activities of the working class—was a suitable workplace for him. He made good use of his talents and excelled in his work. Several years later, he was promoted to the position of deputy director. Nevertheless, his good fortune was reversed when the Cultural Revolution came to an end. As one who was promoted during the Cultural Revolution, he was swiftly purged from his position and had to settle for a job at the city's labor union until his death at the age of sixty-five (Ibid.).

From the vicissitudes of his cousin's life, Teacher Yu learns the lessons of history—"how the fate of a person is closely linked to the fate of the whole nation" and "how a generation was fooled by the age" (Ibid.). He bemoans the lost opportunity of his cousin who was deprived of a university education because "the unified entrance examinations were halted for almost a full decade." He surmises: "My cousin was like so many people of his generation. They should be studying in the universities, and yet they ended up in the countryside. He shouldn't have any problem getting into a university. He had already completed high school, and it was the Number Eight Secondary School (a top school in the city). He was an all-round person" (Ibid.).

It would be difficult to say what kind of a person Dongming would have become if circumstances in his life were different. But Teacher Yu believes that our life trajectories are shaped by different kinds of contextual factors that are embedded in nation's history. As he moved on to fresh undertakings, studying education and graduating from the university, his circumstances were changed by teachers, friends, and colleagues who carried lessons from their own life histories. His decision to remain and work in his *alma mater* reflects one such influence that has affected the course of his life.

STAYING IN THE ACADEME

Teacher Yu graduated from university in the mid-1980s, a period that he terms "an age when Chinese thinking was most open" (Interview 3, 2014: 20). The 1980s was a decade of reconstruction and renewal. China was getting back on its feet again, but it was underdeveloped and lost. Yet, people saw hope in the changes that were made. Promises of resources and freedom gave rise to a kind of optimism that was widely shared among the nation's schools and universities. By the time Teacher Yu graduated from university, the liberalization of economic policies had transformed the job market, and university graduates, who were considered the true elite of the society,[5] actually had a choice of occupation.

For a university graduate like Teacher Yu, there were three career paths to choose at the time: the red route, the gold route, and the black route (Ibid.: 21). "The first route, symbolized by the color red [for ideological rectitude], pointed to the officialdom" (Ibid.). It was the traditional career path for those educated persons who succeeded in the imperial examinations and gained official appointments. Their modern equivalents were the cadres who served in the administration of the party-state. "The second route, symbolized by the color gold [for wealth and prosperity], was taken by graduates who wanted to engage in business" (Ibid.). It offered opportunities for good fortune and promises of a life of comfort and wealth. At the time, it was a path mainly chosen by ambitious graduates whose spirited adventures into the newly found market were metaphorically depicted as "immersing in the sea of commerce." "The third route, represented by the color black [for humility and perseverance] and symbolized by the graduation gown" would lead to a lifelong endeavor in the pursuit of knowledge and truth in the universities or research institutions (Ibid.). It promised nothing more than job security, a humble lifestyle, and relatively higher social status. Teacher Yu chose the black route.

In 1985, Teacher Yu began his job as a student counselor at the university, which was under its Party administration.[6] When he was considered for the position, there was certain skepticism about his suitability that he "was a bit frivolous, bespectacled, fair complexion, none of which were considered strong points for men" (Interview 5, 2016: 3). Nevertheless, at the insistence of his undergraduate class master Mr. Wu Yuqi, he was hired. He worked in student affairs for the next fifteen years. His main duty was the supervision of the daily living of undergraduate students. Teacher Yu thinks that the job put him at the front line of higher education and has benefited his later "research work on education" (Interview 3, 2014: 23). Working as a student counselor afforded him an intimate look at student life on campus and the aspirations, hope, and anxieties of university students. He reflects:

> Being with the students allows me to understand what good education is. It's no longer abstract, no longer conceptual, for every person involved it carries many stories. I believe that when we think of education in terms of humankind, it's supported by tens of thousands of stories. So if we try to understand education without the experience, first-hand experience, it will be hard to fully grasp its meaning. (Ibid.)

In trying to understand the undergraduate students, he read books that were widely read by them because "students were pioneers of the times" (Interview 2, 2014: 1). He tried to solve his students' problems with common sense and tolerance, and modified rules and regulations that seemed unreasonable. He observes that the fifteen years that he spent mingling with young people who "fearlessly and unceasingly embraced the newest ideas and *Zeitgeist*" has allowed him "to feel the pulse of the rapidly changing times" and was "better than reading a hundred books" (Interview 3, 2014: 24, 28).

One example of Teacher Yu's "common sense" approach to student affairs illustrates his amenability to reason and his empathetic understanding of the needs of the students, which led him to bend draconian rules in favor of their well-being. It was in the year 1997 when he was promoted to deputy director of student affairs at the university. The university implemented a series of rules for the undergraduates, including those that forbade them "to put any photo-stickers [of movie stars] on the walls [in their dormitory rooms]"and "hanging their clothing out to dry," but required them "to keep their bedding neatly folded and their luggage tidily stowed" and "to participate in daily morning drills" (Ibid.: 25). The student counselors were charged with the responsibility of ensuring student obedience to the rules. The implementation of these rules had caused considerable dissent among the students who found them to be unreasonable and compliance with them to be difficult.

The bone of contention was the morning drills that the students had to participate in on a daily basis. The morning drills, which harked back to a nationwide program of military training for university freshmen that was introduced several years earlier, were purportedly designed to strengthen the bodies of student-teachers who were destined for a career in teaching. The students queried the logic behind the morning drills by pointing to the absence of their teachers in the exercise: "Why aren't the teachers doing morning drills? We only see some student counselors doing it, but not the teachers. They can still be teachers without having to take part in the morning drills.... When we become teachers in the future, we can avoid the morning drills [like them]. So why do we have to do it now?" (Ibid.).

Teacher Yu thought that the students had a point and waited for an opportunity to manage the discord, perhaps in a more constructive way. The opportunity arose when students from southern China presented a petition to the university's president, asking that the requirement be abolished. The university was situated in the northern part of the country. "Mr. President," the students wrote, "we are students from the southern part of the country, and we have all caught cold whenever we have to run in the morning drills. We are children from the south, and we cannot get use to the [cold] weather in the northeast" (Ibid.). The president sent the student petition to the office of student affairs with the written instruction that "the situation should be examined according to actual circumstances and manage as appropriate" (Ibid.). To Teacher Yu, the president's instruction was like an "imperial sword," a *carte blanche* to handle the grievances with the necessary authority. He reminisces:

> The president wanted us to examine and consider. We considered and abolished the rules. I felt that the students weren't fit enough to get up and do these running drills in the morning, so from then on we didn't require them to go through the drills uniformly. We encouraged them to

participate in the drills, but not uniformly. I've been on the job for over ten years, right?.... Later, we abolished the practice of unified inspection of tidiness and morning drills. That's what I've been saying in my lectures. I kept bringing up this concept, that is, I'm especially against uniformity in education. (Ibid.)

Teacher Yu's experience as a student counselor, "king of children," as adults working with children and youths were commonly called at the time (Ibid.: 28), was rewarding for him. "If I have to do it over again, I'll still choose working with students." He says confidently:

> This is because I studied education and I'm doing research on educa-tion. Student work is fresh. It's doing education every day, mingling with students, figuring out how to teach them, how to work with them, how to guide them and spending time with them. In educational research, if there's no 'doing' in it, then the research will lack vitality. It will lack life. In retrospect, I think my fifteen years in student work is my fifteen years of doing education, fifteen years of doing research on education in the front line, and on site. (Interview 5, 2016: 4)

Teacher Yu's first job in student affairs had something to do with his newly fostered relationship with the Party. He says: "I was just admitted into the Party, and felt that since the organization trusted me, I should go along [with the appointment] and serve its needs. I still retained the traits of people of that generation" (Ibid.: 3). He started as a student counselor, and then moved into areas of work that required more admin-istrative duties. His career path seemed set for that of a Party function-ary whose livelihood was to perform a delicate balancing act between the interests of the Party and the welfare of the students but there were colleagues who had taken an interest in his future, and by nudging him toward academic pursuits, they helped him to carve out a new path of career development.

Mr. Wu, the teacher who had played such an important role in Teacher Yu's first appointment, encouraged him to take on teaching duties. His first teaching assignment was to teach a course on "ideologi-cal and moral education," which was a required university-level course for all undergraduates. Teacher Yu looks back on the dawn of his teach-ing career:

It was the kind of course that many teachers considered beneath them. It was a hard course to teach. The students didn't think they needed it. They knew that you were lecturing them on how to establish goals in life, on the concept of love, on what an ideal job is and on the kind of person that you wanted them to be. Actually, it put you in an embarrassing position. The course wasn't a part of any major, and it wasn't a foreign language course. You had to find some way to make it attractive to them. This experience let me understand first-hand the art of education: what is good teaching, what good education is, and how to be a good teacher. Thinking back, I see teaching this course on ideology and moral education for over ten years as a kind of capital investment for me. To be a good teacher, one needs to figure out how to teach the course well, and how to grip the students. What you say may be the truth, but they don't want to listen. Your course may even be considered a negative part in the curriculum. This decade-long experience has affected me up to this day. I think that if a person in educational research cannot teach well, cannot attract students, then he's less than perfect, flawed. (Interview 2, 2014: 8–9)

In teaching a university-level required course which was designed to foster the political rectitude of undergraduate students, Teacher Yu seemed able to handle the pedagogical problems that had discouraged many of his colleagues. He attributes his teaching performance to an understanding of the students: "What are the interests of students? You've got to find out what excites them, including their motivation in learning. So when I taught this course, I paid special attention to the books that they read, and the latest academic discussions on thinking, on ethics, and on the psychological development of young people" (Interview 5, 2016: 3). He also attributes his ability to capture the attention of students to his student counseling experience:

I had a thorough understanding of the students and their needs. The good thing about doing student work is that it let me understand the students. This is a prerequisite for good teaching. What is it that you say that the students are willing to listen to? How do you make them listen to you? If they really don't listen, they won't be able to learn anything in an English language course. But that's not the case for a moral education course.... If you don't understand [your students], you won't be good in teaching. I believe in what Chairman Mao had once said, that when we eat, we have to know how much food is on the table; when we make clothing, we have to know the size of the wearer; and when we sing, we have to know the [inhabitants of the] mountains where our songs would be heard. The same applies to education and to teaching. (Interview 3, 2014: 24)

In addition to teaching, Teacher Yu also started to pay attention to research and to writing. Again, it was his teacher Mr. Wu Yuqi who recommended diversity in his career building. "Mr. Wu told me that there were three things that I needed to do. The first thing to do is to learn English. Whatever test you have to take in the future, English will be included." Teacher Yu enumerates his teacher's instruction: "The second is to do research. You have to do research no matter what. The third is to teach. If you can accomplish all three, you can do anything." And, as if accounting for his accomplishments, he speculates: "Of the three things [that I was supposed to do], my perseverance in learning English was so-so, not like the efforts that I've put into writing, studying, and teaching. I think if I had put in more effort then, my English should be much better now" (Interview 3, 2014: 28).

IDENTITY ISSUE 1: WHAT AM I?

Aside from the advice of Mr. Wu, Teacher Yu also benefitted from the training that another teacher, Mr. Liu Hezhong, had given him. The training was in writing, particularly the writing of work reports for the organization. Mr. Liu was a senior political educator at the university, serving as the secretary general of the Communist Youth League (the junior partner of the Chinese Communist Party devoted to preparing youths to join the Party). He was well-versed in matters related to official documents. Teacher Yu gratefully acknowledges his mentorship: "It was under the instruction of [Mr. Liu] that I began writing important materials and lengthy work reports at the age of twenty-two or twenty-three. The writing also included academic essays. Mr. Liu was the teacher who initiated me into writing. He was the reason why I could write all these things later on" (Interview 5, 2016: 3).

Under the supervision of Messrs. Wu and Liu, Teacher Yu learned the skills required for academic work. He also got to know the workings of the Party organization. Nevertheless, there seemed to be a tension in his career. It concerned the status of his student counselor position in the university. He recalls:

The nature of my identity was embarrassing. By taking up the job as a secretary in the office of the Communist Youth League, some said that you were an administrator but people in the university administration said that you were a political worker. I didn't understand the difference when I decided to stay and work here. If you want me to be a League secretary, I'd be a League secretary. At the time I didn't know what a League secretary had to do. I thought that it was nice to stay in the university and work as a League secretary. The teachers trusted me. But when I reported to work, they said that I was a political worker. I asked them what a political worker was. I didn't understand. (Interview 3, 2014: 28)

Teacher Yu later found out that his position was neither in the academic stream nor the administrative stream of the university administration. His job as a student counselor was categorized as a "political worker" (*zhenggong*) who worked under the direction of the Party that operated with self-governing authority on campus. As a Party functionary, he was supposed to ensure political rectitude and proper behavior of the students. The course that he taught on ideology and moral education was offered by the "office of research on moral education" as an integral part of the undergraduate curriculum (Interview 5, 2016: 3), but its content and methods were controlled by the Party. He worked in a zone of marginality for many years, and, in spite of his gradual advancement within the Party organization, the problem of identity continued to bewilder him (Interview 3, 2014: 28).

For Teacher Yu, the thorny problem of station was perhaps the major misgiving that never ceased to nag him. "What is my identity in this university? An administrator? A faculty member?" were recurring questions that he kept asking himself. Later, it became clear to him that "being a student counselor differed from being a teacher, because the identities were different." He explains: "Those who served as teachers were called 'professional teachers' or 'full-time teachers'. We were called 'staff of student political work'. Later, I actually felt something and that was, in the eyes of some teachers, being a political worker was lower in status, a kind of connotation like administrative staff" (Interview 5, 2016: 3). The rude awakening to lower work status caused Teacher Yu's first identity crisis: "It was a letdown, let me tell you, it was a letdown. It was an identity crisis. There were people in the society who didn't look up to those doing my kind of work" (Interview 3, 2014: 28).

EMERGENCE OF SCHOLARLY LIFE

Identity crisis notwithstanding, Teacher Yu remained in student affairs and continued to explore opportunities in the academic stream. His scholarly endeavor began in earnest at the turn of the century when he formally started his study of the philosophy of education. He finally got a chance to enroll in a doctoral program, a pursuit that would eventually prove to be a vital link for crossing the border from political work to academic work.

At the advent of the twenty-first century, Teacher Yu was making impressive progress in his career. His ascension to the position of Party Secretary of the Faculty of Education (the political counterpart of the dean of faculty) elevated his status in the university. It also gave him an opportunity to influence the policy direction of the university in the fluid environment of higher education where expansion and reform were the order of the day. His teaching seemed to be appreciated by students, and he had ventured beyond political education by teaching other courses in "educational studies" (Interview 5, 2016: 3). He published enough academic articles to qualify for a full professorship in 1998 (Ibid.: 4). However, without further study in a formal discipline, he would remain a political worker wandering about on the outskirts of scholarship. For him, the doctoral study that began in 2002 was an essential and inevitable step toward forging a new identity.

Teacher Yu pursued his doctoral study in the philosophy of education under the supervision of a prominent scholar, Prof. Wang Fengxian.[7] He is proud to be the student of a scholar of exceptional status and a teacher who was also an exemplar of academic freedom and moral courage. He remembers his late supervisor with a mixture of admiration, for his accomplishments, and sympathy, for the hardship that he suffered during the Cultural Revolution and afterward:

> It was in the 1980s when Professor Wang was severely criticized for insisting on his own points of view [which were contrary to those of the powers-that-be]. I could see that his face was puffy when he gave a lecture to us. It was in 1983 when he taught us 'theories of moral education'. His face was puffy. It was right after [one of these sessions where] he endured criticisms. It was a kind of political criticism. He had endured ten years of Cultural Revolution. If you're wearing the 'dunces cap', your whole family and even marriage would be greatly affected. It wasn't about problems in your scholarship. Your survival would be met with a lot of challenges. But

we have much more academic freedom now than in those days. (Interview 1, 2009: 3)

Throughout his doctoral study, Teacher Yu had remained faithful to his role of a student in spite of his growing status in administration. One example of his constancy was the choice of topic for his doctoral thesis, which was on modernity, postmodernism, and education. The choice was made by his supervisor after some discussion between mentor and student. Teacher Yu had wanted to write his thesis on an aspect of the Cultural Revolution because of its far-reaching effects and the dearth of publications on the period in the Chinese Mainland. Professor Wang did not agree to the topic because he thought "it was too sensitive a topic that would involve historic figures and the personal interests of those who were still alive" (Ibid.). Teacher Yu's other choice was to examine the educational thought of Mao Zedong, whom he considered to be the most influential figure in contemporary Chinese education. Yet, there were strict limitations on the research of this kind. What one could or could not say placed serious constraints on scholarly research. At the suggestion of Prof. Wang, he finally settled on modernity, postmodernism, and education as a topic for his thesis "because my teacher was concerned about postmodernism" (Interview 2, 2014: 2) and thought that postmodernism would challenge the existing "rules" of education in China. "It was something that he was worrying about" (Ibid.: 7).

Like most doctoral students in the Chinese tradition, Teacher Yu accepted his teacher's suggestion dutifully (Ibid.: 2–3).[8] His ready acceptance of an assigned area of study was natural in the Chinese academic context, for rejecting such an assignment would be taken as a sign of disrespect that would cause tension in the mentor–student relationship that was supposed to last a lifetime. In Chinese academia, where the will of senior academics often prevailed over the personal interests of young scholars, the latter often altered their research focuses after they began their academic careers. Frequently, their original academic interests, nurtured by doctoral study, were modified or even abandoned in favor of the prevailing interests of their departments.[9] During his tenure, Teacher Yu did not have to compromise his interest in postmodernism even when it was on the periphery of mainstream departmental pursuits. His independence was probably due to the fact that he was already an established administrator-teacher in the faculty at the time.

By the time when he completed his doctoral thesis, which was entitled "Modernity and Education—Modernity, Anxiety and Philosophical Response in the Context of Postmodernism," he had started to gather a sizable collection of works by the masters of postmodernism and Western philosophy. He is proud of this collection of books and would indulge his passion for them in the presence of students and visitors. His interest in postmodernism continued to grow and became an important part of his scholarly identity.

An interesting fact about Teacher Yu's intellectual growth is that his interest in postmodernism actually preceded his interest in modernity. "I knew about the term ['postmodernism'] before I knew what modernity meant," he says (Interview 5, 2016: 5). He was reading Foucault before his supervisor assigned the topic of his doctoral thesis. He also read "the works of Lyotard, Derrida, Jamieson, Dole, and Pinar." Pinar's lecture at his university in the year 2000 provided the impetus for his further exploration (Ibid.). Teacher Yu saw postmodernism as a reflection and critique of modernist rationality, and considered rationality a major epistemological component in the foundation of education. He explains:

After a long period of material collection, thinking and reflection, I felt that modernity was a topic worthy of study. In the realm of educational studies, there aren't a lot of publications on modernity in this country or abroad. This is especially true for research on modernity and education. So with the agreement of Professor Wang, I chose to analyze issues pertaining to the performance, effects and way forward for modernity in education under the influence of postmodernism. (Ibid.)

His mentor Prof. Wang had played an important role in Teacher Yu's scholarly development by selecting a thesis topic that set him on a sustained course of inquiry. Professor Wang suffered from political repression because he was determined to speak his mind. His insistence that Teacher Yu's thesis topic should not be politically "sensitive" or one that could affect "the personal interests of those who were still alive" (Interview 1, 2009: 3) could be his way of protecting his student from suffering his own misfortune over again. History might repeat itself in strange ways, and it would be inadvisable to expound politically controversial matters in one's work. Such exposition would be difficult to avoid if Teacher Yu had chosen either the Cultural Revolution or the educational thought of Mao Zedong as the topic of his thesis. Professor Wang was mindful of the pitfalls of veracious scholarship, so an exploratory exercise in the novel field of postmodernism seemed like a safe endeavor for his student at the time.

Professor Wang was also important to Teacher Yu's professional development by guiding him to an understanding of the effects that important stakeholders have had on Chinese education. To him, the dynamics among these educational stakeholders actually affected the direction and quality of educational discourse in China. Teacher Yu explicates his mentor's rationale:

> My teacher Wang Fengxian once said, 'We need to consider three groups of people when we try to understand the thinking behind Chinese education. The first group consists of those in educational administration, the so-called educational officials. What are they thinking? They are the decision-makers and executives in education. The second group consists of the frontline [school] principals and teachers. They are the actors, the implementers in education. What are they thinking? Finally, the third group is us, the so-called researchers in research institutes and higher institutions. What are we thinking? And what ideas have we produced?' I think whatever these three groups of people are thinking will, to a certain extent, affect the kind of educational reform that we shall have in China. (Interview 2, 2014: 3)

As Teacher Yu realized, the attention given to the views of these three kinds of stakeholders would yield a comprehensive understanding of Chinese education. In his attempt to "do" educational research, he would have to go further into the field of practice in order to gain an appreciation of the changes that have occurred in the country's education and to foster ideas that are relevant to its reality.

COMBINING SCHOLARSHIP AND ADMINISTRATION

Once Teacher Yu became the Party Secretary of the Faculty of Education, his career path was steered into the site of university administration. His promotion to a full professorship in Education Theory had given him an academic home, but his identity in the faculty seemed to be tagged to his Party position. For one who has professed an inclination toward academic work, either for status or intellectual reasons, he had to make the conversion from political work to academic labor.

The conversion was not easy, for he had to play the roles of an administrator and a scholar simultaneously in order to remain in the academic stream. He had taken the longer route to reach his goal, and he had made it possible by a steady demonstration of administrative leadership. Interestingly, as his career as an academic unfolded, his identity as an officer in university administration came into sharper focus. This ironic sway of identity was mostly due to consecutive assignments that brought him into leadership positions in research, distance education, and faculty management.

In 2005, the year when Teacher Yu completed his doctoral study, he was appointed as the director of an established research institute that was devoted to the study of rural education. He served in that position for two-and-a-half years. The university's Rural Education Research Institute was considered a national stronghold for the study of rural education, a key indicator of the country's overall educational development. Being the head of such a unit had allowed Teacher Yu to "get close to the countryside, pay it serious attention, study and understand the countryside. It allowed me to feel [the pulse of] Chinese education intuitively and directly," he says (Interview 5, 2016: 4). With the new appointment, he could observe in close-up the educational problems that had frustrated development efforts in the rural areas. He reflects on his work at the institute:

> Rural education is a problem area in Chinese education. What are its intransigent problems? Or, what does it mean to have a kind of education that is indigenously Chinese? After serving for two years as institute director, I deepened my personal experience in [rural education]. [I realized that] in my mind's eye, "the countryside" was only an abstract term, and rural education was just an abstract figure. After paying over nine visits to rural secondary and primary schools, and also talking to the rural workers at construction sites to find out about their education, I understood what it was like to receive education in the rural areas. Those cold abstractions came alive for me. That's why I've often had this sensitivity for "indigenization" and [was able to be] "on-site" in my research. It's related to these two years of experience. (Ibid.)

In his attempt to make sense of the influence of local conditions on education, Teacher Yu also became aware of the constraints that they imposed. For rural areas that have been burdened by perpetual poverty, the benefits of education were often overshadowed by the lure of economic gains. Teacher Yu recalls an encounter with a young person during one of his field trips:

> There are kids who won't go to school even when they're [already] ten years old. Just working, making money ... I've asked a kid about this. I said: 'There are all these government subsidies now. You don't have to pay [school fees], and you can receive [government] subsidy every day [if you go to school]. Students in boarding school will also get subsidized. So why aren't you in school?' The boy replied: 'I won't go [to school] even if it's free, because it affects my chance of making money.' That's why I feel that it's so difficult to have compulsory education for the whole country. (Ibid.: 6)

Teacher Yu's tenure at the research institute was short. His most memorable moment was the insights he gained during a 2006 study trip to Yan'an, the "Mecca" of Chinese communist revolution. The ten-day trip was arranged during his two-month study at the Central Party School. It was an eye-opener for him. In Yan'an, his visits to the cadre college, the museums, and the former residence of Chairman Mao called attention to the lessons of the revolution and the meaning of being "indigenously Chinese." He says: "Before [my visit to Yan'an], I wasn't very cognizant of matters related to the 'old liberation region', Mao Zedong, indigenization, and sinicization. Of course we all talked about them. It's often like that: when other people talk about something that they all consider important, but you don't have an acute awareness of it, then it's as though it doesn't really exist" (Interview 1, 2009: 2). But the milieu of Yan'an, its atmosphere, artifacts, music, and dance changed that for Teacher Yu. He was particularly impressed by the writings of Mao whose ideas of "sinicization, Chinese characteristics, Chinese Aura were clarified during my stay in Yan'an" (Interview 5, 2016: 5). He shares the revelation:

> In Yan'an, I developed a deeper appreciation of sinicization and indigenization. Why was Mao Zedong able to guide the Chinese revolution to a successful conclusion?.... One important factor was that Mao Zedong had given Chinese culture, Chinese countryside, Chinese peasants, and Chinese revolution his deep and thorough consideration. That was why the strategies and policies that he proposed had won the hearts of the

people and suited the thinking of the times. That was why they were effective. (Ibid.)

Shortly after Teacher Yu returned to the university, he was reassigned to a position that was more entrepreneurial than academic. In 2007, he took up the directorship of the university's School of Distance Education and remained there for five years. In the same year, he was promoted to the level of "assistant to the president" (Ibid.), a generic job title that was equivalent to that of a vice-president at the university. For the university, the School of Distance Education was an auxiliary arm that offered revenue-generating extension programs. It was considered an important money-making unit. The School operated a variety of training programs for working professionals, including professional development courses for school teachers. At the time, the national government had just launched a massive nationwide project to retrain teachers for the curriculum reform in schools.

While serving as the head of distance education, Teacher Yu continued to teach courses in Education Theory, including "basic theories, education of philosophy, and readings in selected topics" (Ibid.: 4) and supervised graduate students. However, given all that he had to do, one wonders how much time was allowed for serious engagement in scholarship. As the School's director, Teacher Yu was responsible for initiating and managing a variety of extension courses for a large number of students. He estimated that "there were about seventy thousand students learning through the Internet [in the programs of his unit]; and, at the time, the student enrollment of the whole university was between twenty and thirty thousand students" (Ibid.). Despite the huge subscription, it was his duty to create more business opportunities for the School. His chief mission was to dispel public skepticism toward distance education, a form of education that employed a pedagogical mode that made it vulnerable to cheating. He asserts:

> This kind of [distance] learning is free from the constraint of time and space, … and the entry requirements are not high. [Its] whole process is done on the Internet. Admission, counseling, tutorial advise, and examination are all done on the Internet. There are people who doubt its reliability. They suspect that there may be cheating going on. But with the gradual improvement of technologies, there should be less and less cheating. It's like buying books on the Internet. We use [electronic] banking

and 'Alipay' (the equivalent of 'PayPal' in China). There were people who questioned [its reliability] at first. But when it is widely used and there's no problem, then people will be assured. (Ibid.)

Teacher Yu's interest in distance education was heightened by the impressive growth in the subscription of school teachers to the university's training programs. He explains: "At the time, an important function of the School of Distance Education was the training of in-service teachers. There were several thousand teachers enrolled [at the university] for training every year. When I assumed the directorship, we were running about ten classes in a year. By the time I left office, we operated about seventy classes per year" (Ibid.). For him, personally, his involvement in teacher training afforded him a chance to develop through the "growing contact with front-line principals and teachers, which sensitized and familiarized me with the situation of school reform" (Ibid.).

The appointments to the directorship of the research institute and of distance education had changed the course of work for Teacher Yu. The seven years of varied experiences as the head of two important units of the university was an adventure for a political educator who, only ten years ago, was pondering an appropriate topic for his doctoral thesis. Given the logic of Chinese organization, it might perhaps be assumed that his career advancement was due in part to his move into administrative work that he had worked his way into "leadership positions" by taking the administrative route in the organization. Clearly, from the time he took up the directorship of distance education, his career was anchored in the sea of administration. However, there was a brief period of two years when he could play the dual role of scholar and administrator again, a situation similar to his tenure at the research institute. Only this time, he was asked to return to the Faculty of Education and to lead it to a new and higher level of development.

LEADING A "FIVE-STAR UNIT"

Teacher Yu returned to the Faculty of Education as its dean in 2012. The appointment signified the university's recognition of his leadership ability by placing under his charge a unit that had played a central role in helping it to fulfill its core mission as a normal university. For over a decade, the university was lauded for its adherence to its original mission of nurturing teachers, while other top normal universities had suffered from a mission drift by trying to transform themselves into comprehensive universities. The Faculty of Education was a showcase for the university, not only for signifying its unwavering stance in teacher education but also for demonstrating its achievements in educational studies. Teacher Yu was proud to be the head of such a unit. He spells out its strengths:

> Our Faculty of Education is a five-star unit of the university. The reason why it's a five-star unit is because it houses key disciplines that are recognized nationally, and it also has postdoctoral programs and key institutes. So its strengths stand out. Actually, as a discipline, our educational studies had always been ranked amongst the best in the Nation. (Interview 5, 2016: 4)

His delight notwithstanding, the new appointment had caused anxiety for Teacher Yu who had to maintain the high status of his faculty at the university. He admits: "Some people said that the Faculty of Education was the most important faculty [of the university]. I think there's some truth to it" (Ibid.). Thus, every plan that he formulated and every decision he made in the faculty would reflect not only his leadership ability but also his personal vision of his future ambitions for the faculty. Moreover, the deanship required an experienced educator with a solid scholarly background so that the faculty's image in the education sector could be enhanced. Teacher Yu's predecessor, a reputable scholar in curriculum and teaching, possessed the kind of attributes that fit such an image well. An academic who was well known in the field and well liked by his colleagues, he left behind ten years of accomplishments that his successor felt challenged to emulate.

One of Teacher Yu's first major tasks as Dean was to establish a clear identity for his colleagues in the world of scholarship. He ponders:

> What is it that distinguishes our educational research? For example, Beijing Normal University, East China Normal University, and Nanjing Normal University all have 'Educational Theory'. So what kind of research are we going to do for our 'Educational Theory' here? Clearly we can't simply replicate what others are doing. Our research may somewhat overlap with what they do in Beijing, but what kind of research is something that we *have* to do here? The same kind of questions surfaced after our discussion with colleagues [of the same field] working in other institutions. The construction of an academic discipline has to do with its special characteristics. In the absence of such characteristics, we'll lack core competitiveness.

So the first question that I asked when I became dean was how we could inherit the great legacies [of our university] in discipline construction. Or, should I say, what kind of research have we done in the last sixty years? And what kind of research should we do in order to foster core competitiveness, make it sustainable, and keep enhancing the quality of our scholarship and our work in nurturing talents. These are the questions that have concerned me in the last two years. (Ibid.: 5)

In setting a new course of development for his faculty, Teacher Yu realized that, as a faculty of education, it had to forge closer linkage with the schools, and that its research had to be directed toward the "educational front-line." He recalls: "So during my deanship, I worked with the [municipal government] to establish a research unit for basic education ... and I visited over fifty schools, giving lectures and engaging in exchange, during those two years" (Ibid.).

Another key area of his work was the internationalization of the faculty so that its research and academic programs "can face the world and have an international outlook." The first step toward internationalization was to strengthen its academic exchange. He recounts: "So during this period I invited Pinar to come [to the university] to give lectures. I also visited the university of British Columbia, and went to the U.S. and Japan for exchange. This is because a first-rate university should not only have a passion for its own culture and its unique character, but also an international outlook" (Ibid.).

In his vision for the faculty, Teacher Yu seemed most concerned about the kind of values that would guide it to the next stage of development. Higher education in China has changed significantly in the new century. After a massive expansion in student enrollment, the top universities were given extra resources to raise their quality to "world-class" status. The universities were classified and ranked in accordance with their functions, status, and performance, institution by institution, and discipline by discipline. Research and publication were given tremendous emphasis in developmental strategies and in personnel decisions. With more and more students going abroad for their university education, Chinese higher institutions have had to, for the first time in their existence, compete with overseas universities for students of their own country. These changes made it imperative for the Faculty of Education to transform itself in order to keep pace with the growing demands of the times. To confront these changes, Teacher Yu deferred to traditional wisdom for an axiological anchor for the endeavors of the faculty. He suggests:

> There are three sentences in *Zhongyong* (*Book of the Mean*) that represent the core of educational philosophy in China. We could use it as our spiritual guide. The core states that education must be appropriate to human nature. It says: 'What Heaven confers is called "nature." Accordance with this nature is called the Way. Cultivating the Way is called education.' ... Education needs to be conducted in accordance with human nature. I believe that it delineates the basis of education.

Teacher Yu wanted to use this notation of traditional wisdom as the motto of the Faculty of Education. He pledges:

> For the graduating class [of next year], I'll have these sentences engraved on stone. Whoever wants to look at it can look at it. I'll have [the stone] put on the most prominent spot. The spirit of our Faculty will be based on 'Accordance with nature is called the Way. Cultivating the Way is called education (ten characters).' They will be on the name cards of the colleagues here. And I want to use the style of the *Zhuan* characters (an ancient style of Chinese calligraphy often used on seals) for the engraving, not the usual white characters. I want the calligraphy to depict culture, to have certain flavor to it. (Interview 2, 2014: 6–7)

Venturing Back to School

If it were Teacher Yu's intention to leave his intellectual footprint by leaving the engraved motto on the doorstep of the Faculty, its impression would be light. He served as the dean of education for only two years. Then, a personnel reshuffle, which occurred shortly after he played host to Pinar's visit in 2014, caused him to move on again. The new appointment was the principalship of one of the university's affiliated primary schools, an elite school that was widely considered to be an exemplar of primary education in the city. The appointment surprised Teacher Yu. He calls to mind the assignment:

> Frankly, the appointment to the affiliated primary school came as a surprise to me. I remember it was on July 11, 2014. I was with my students, having lunch. I was awarded a special professorial title by the provincial authorities that day. We were still eating, and then there was a call from

the university that said the key leaders wanted to talk to me. I didn't know what it was about. Then I met with the Party secretary and the president of the university. They said 'the university had decided to send you to the affiliated primary school to be its principal.' They said that there's no condition attached. They wanted unconditional compliance. So this appointment was not in my plans, absolutely not. I never dreamt that I would be working in the primary school. The university [leaders] felt that the primary school was important. They also offer me the job of 'assistant to the president'. Actually, before this [appointment], I was already on the grade level of 'assistant to the president' from 2007. Only this time, I was offered a substantive position. (Interview 5, 2016: 5)

The university's affiliated primary school was the kind of school with space and facilities that compared favorably to Teacher Yu's faculty. He seemed to have adapted well to the role of the school principal in the new workplace. Visitors saw him at the school gates at the end of the school day, seeing his students off and making sure that they left in an orderly fashion. He strolled along the corridors of the school, observing the activities that went on in its specialist classrooms—music and art rooms, language learning facilities, canteens, and so on. He moved into a smaller space so that the original oversized principal's office could be converted it into a conference room for meetings of study groups and for staff development activities. He wanted to "facilitate family-school cooperation" and to "find a way to let parents play an important part in the improvement of the school" (Interview 4, 2014: 12). He reviewed the school's curriculum and tried to enrich it and make it more relevant to the life of his students. He advocated a collective effort by the whole staff to forge a new understanding of the students:

I talked to the teachers of the school and said, 'The first thing we need to do is to seriously study the psychology of the children, that is, their psychological development. We need to thoroughly study and understand what the children's needs are. What is it that they can accept? What kind of ways [of learning] do they like?' We should really learn from the doctors, learn from the nutritionists. From my personal observation, I think that our schools today really aren't doing much for our understanding of children. A lot of people simply [perform their teaching] from experience. (Ibid.)

The role of a school principal was novel to Teacher Yu whose work experience was exclusively in higher education. However, he was unfazed by the fact that he was a novice in school education. He says:

> My mission [in the school] is not only to put things into practice, but also to reflect and to conduct research.... As the principal, I have proposed an important concept which is close to the reality of China. It is the concept of 'education in accordance with the nature of the child (*shuaixing jiaoyu*)'. 'Nature' is traced back to *Zhongyong* (*Book of the Mean*): first, protect the nature of the children.... Secondly, respect their inborn nature, their differences, and their imperfections. Thirdly, nurture an understanding of their place in society, cultivate their cultural understanding, core literacy, and let them have an awareness of rules and responsibility, as well as self-understanding and tolerance. (Interview 5, 2016: 7)

Teacher Yu's advocacy for the principle of "education in accordance with the nature of the child" was consistent with his view on teacher education when he was serving as the dean of education. It reflected his belief in Confucian teachings that cultivating the natural mental and emotional constitution of the person is the most natural approach to education. Nevertheless, Teacher Yu did not elaborate on the philosophical basis of his recommendation for "natural education." There was no clear indication that he was ready to defend Mencius' position on the innate goodness of the person, nor did he assume that his teachers could safeguard the blissful state of their students' nature, like the tutor in Rousseau's *Emile*, against the corrupting forces of society.

In reality, Teacher Yu and the teachers in his school, if they were to support his approach to education, would have to strive to reach their goal in an education system where officials and parents seek quick results rather than laudable ideas, and where the meritocracy that it seeks to build is based on performance in examinations. The absence of plausible specifics in Teacher Yu's recommendation gave the impression that the proposed approach was a reflection of his core educational values rather than a blueprint for implementation. However, by projecting the fruit of his work to the future of his students, Teacher Yu seemed hopeful. He speculates: "This primary school is an experimental school. If I could use my position [as school principal] to initiate reform experiments that would lay an important foundation for the future development of my students, like their character and cultural literacy, and if I could do a good job in this, then I would be able to contribute my share to basic education in China" (Ibid.).

People at the university were all surprised when Teacher Yu was assigned to the headship of the primary school. Speculations abound as to why he had traded the lecture halls of the university for the classrooms of a primary school. The one reason that most observers seemed to agree on was that the university needed his service urgently; only this time, it was to fill the position that was vacated by the sudden departure of the former principal of the school. By conforming to the university's decision on personnel deployment "unconditionally," Teacher Yu was able to demonstrate his capability in handling the demands arising from a broad range of positions. Having been appointed to positions that ran the gamut from research director to head of distance education, and from faculty dean to school principal, he has aptly met the challenges of a range of diverse jobs and accumulated valuable professional capital along the way.

IDENTITY ISSUE 2: WHAT AM I DOING?

Even when his career journey had led him to posts of different orientations, Teacher Yu remained faithful to his scholarly pursuits. He continued to teach at the Faculty of Education and supervised graduate students. He was engaged in research projects and published books and journal papers. His interest in postmodernism and education has not waned, even though he has added other interests to his analysis of educational issues, such as equality and sustainable development. Ironically, his continuous involvement in scholarship has cast doubts on the meaning of his pursuits. This time, it was an identity issue that emerged from his perplexity over the nature and functions of the philosophy of education and his own role as an intellectual and an educator in the changing context of China.

Teacher Yu's second identity problem—the first being the dubious status of his position as a "political worker"—stemmed from his growing awareness of the chasm between ideas and practice that existed in the highly contested field of education. He acknowledges the limitations of scholarship in the "real world": "You can't expect to change the reality with an essay" (Interview 3, 2014: 13). He also knew that, in the reality of China, a person's official position far outweighed his scholarly achievements. "So 'academic democracy, scholar centeredness' has a long way to go in China," he says, "In their absence, Chinese research won't be able to forge ahead healthily" (Interview 2, 2014: 10). In trying to shed light on his own identity problem, Teacher Yu reverted back to a familiar problem in the field of philosophy of education. He queries:

> What is philosophy of education? This is a very big bewilderment, really. Some would say that it is analyzing education from a philosophical perspective. So is it talking philosophically at length, add some educational issues, and then call it philosophy of education? [My mentor Wang Fengxian] pointed out that issues in philosophy of education and theories of philosophy of education should originate from the field of education and not just through the transference of philosophical theories ... Education is not a colony of philosophy, nor is it a dependent on philosophy. (Interview 3, 2014: 28–29)

As a scholar in the field, Teacher Yu was keenly aware of philosophy's fading relevance to education because of its inability to address educational issues "in the Chinese context" and its aloofness from educational practice. To him, the same can be said about the theory-building efforts for education in China. The construction of educational theories is "based on concepts, theories and principles rather than on real education that is alive, education with flesh and blood. Facts of the education world are simply used as examples to explicate certain theories" (Yu and Qin 2009: 28). Given their detachment from the field, the purpose of educational theories is being questioned, but they "continue to multiply without benefitting the effectiveness of indigenous educational practice" (Ibid.).

For Teacher Yu, a scholar who has based his inquiry on such Western theorists as Marx, Lyotard, Foucault, Bourdieu, Giddens, and Pinar (Interview 3, 2014: 11–13), his identity problem was further delineated by an arduous process of "border-crossing," from being a "romantic" to being a "pragmatist." In the Chinese context, these terms should be understood as a rough categorization of sociopolitical persuasions among Chinese intellectuals who have viewed the developmental course of China through different ideological and strategic lenses. To Teacher Yu, being "romantic" is to create a good vision in one's mind, paint a good picture for that vision, even portray it poetically, and call for societal change without confronting the deeply rooted problems or trying to solve them in a constructive way (Interview 3, 2014: 16).

Looking back on his own intellectual journey, Teacher Yu reminisces: "I used to be a romantic, but I am not a romantic now. I realized that if you want to understand education in China you can't just be romantic, you need feasible methods, something more rigorous" (Interview 2, 2014: 14). He pointed to the limitations of lofty ideals: "We can't simply look at things from the perspectives of philosophy and poetry. They can help you fly up to the sky; but they would have a hard time helping you to come down to earth. It may be possible to have an exceptional person who can fly up to the sky; but we can't require everyone to do the same, for that would be disastrous" (Interview 3, 2014: 17). To illustrate his point, Teacher Yu alluded to the calamitous Great Leap Forward in the late 1950s, a failed nationwide campaign that aimed to propel China's overall economic production to an unprecedented height in a very short time. He calls to mind his teacher's sober admonishment:

My mentor once remarked that the Great Leap Forward in 1958 and many things done thereafter were based on the thinking of a poet.[10] We hoped that China could become a Communist country and a global steel producer overnight. It didn't work.... I admit that we need to have ideals, even a utopian [vision] for education. But when it comes to policies [to be implemented] on a systemic level, it is important that we be practical, be more conservative. We should take our time and not be too hasty. (Ibid.)

The "romantics," for Teacher Yu, "build their conception on ideals, treat human beings as human beings. They stop at the individual level. But this is not enough, for without the support of institutional measures, the best [intentions] may not lead to the best conditions. It may even lead to iniquity. At worst, romantics only remain at the level of invocations. If they stay that way, without being transformed into institutions and policies, they will forever remain romantic callings" (Interview 4, 2014: 13).

Teacher Yu's conversion to a more pragmatic worldview began when his work led him away from the cloistered life of the university and to the site of policy implementation. In the field of educational practice where he worked as a researcher and a school principal, he developed a firmer grasp of the meaning of policy constraints as he observed the drag of lofty plans and blind zealotry on implementation, and how well-intentioned but ill-conceived plans could easily go astray. Moreover, the intellectual impetus for his adopting a pragmatic approach was through reading Marx (Ibid.: 14). He reasons: "Marx's background was in law, and he spent forty years studying economics.... Both disciplines are intimately tied to the real and direct interests of people" (Ibid.: 13). By citing Lu Xun, a prominent writer in modern China, Teacher Yu argues that "[reading] Marx affords a frank depiction of the dismal conditions of human life." He recounts his intellectual debt to Marx:

> Marx is like a doctor, confronting the disease, and uses his knife to dissect it carefully. What are the actual causes of the sufferings of the poor? Why is our society filled with wickedness? ... [Marx's thinking] gives me a strong sense of reality. In analyzing China's education, we should not simply confine ourselves to issues in education, but examine educational issues from social, political, and economic perspectives. Only then can you possibly analyze and explain them clearly. (Ibid.)

The conversion allowed Teacher Yu to consider the practicality and feasibility of educational policies. "Being practical" is now a term that he uses for self-depiction, which is frequently uttered with a faint sigh. He uses as an example of "being practical" a fanciful account of an exchange that allegedly took place between Jimmy Carter, the president of the USA, and Deng Xiaoping, the architect of China's Open Door Policy:

> During his visit to China in the 1970s, Carter said to Deng Xiaoping: 'You don't have human rights in China, and why is it so difficult for the Chinese people to go to America?' Deng replied: 'Okay, I'll allow thirty million people to go to America tomorrow.' But Carter said that it wouldn't do because there wouldn't be enough space to accommodate all these people. You see, there are things that sound good theoretically; but when you have to really do it, you've got to consider the reality ... consider the feasibility. If you only think in terms of ideals, your action may bring disaster. (Interview 3, 2014: 16–17)

In a sense, Teacher Yu's conversion may have been expedited by his appointment to positions of substantial administrative responsibilities. As an implementer of educational policies, he has grown increasingly aware of the demands that required him to be practical and to devise feasible ways of delivering results: respectable output by the research institute; extra income for the university through distance education; enhanced institutional profile for the faculty; and impressive improvement of the primary school. In playing his roles as researcher, educational entrepreneur, and academic administrator, Teacher Yu had to learn to think and act pragmatically in order to endure the trials of administration and policy implementation. Perhaps it was the intellectual in him who was sighing when he confessed to "being more practical than before." He has played his roles well. Whether it was his empathy that he seemed to have inherited from his ancestors, or his insistence on sustaining his scholarly pursuits, or his ability to simply seize favorable opportunities in his life, his ascension up the ladder of the university hierarchy is an indication that he and his efforts were appreciated.

As a Chinese intellectual, however, Teacher Yu may have mixed feelings about reaping the benefits of his worldly wisdom rather than adhering to the traditions of the Chinese intelligentsia—from being the idealistic change agents of the May Fourth Movement to being the critical cultural rejuvenators at the turn of the century.[11] No matter the source of his misgivings, Teacher Yu's views on China's situation at the crossroads of tradition and modernity, as well as its struggle to balance the foreign and the indigenous, should shed further light on the pathway of his intellectual change as well as the educational circumstances that surround it.

Notes

1. In China, a "normal university" is a higher education institution that is or was devoted to the education of teachers and the advancement of knowledge in academic disciplines that are related to the subjects of the school curriculum. When the country's comprehensive universities began to offer teacher education programs by establishing units for educational studies and teacher education, the "normal universities" changed their orientation and broadened their curricula and course offerings. Today, major "normal universities" resemble comprehensive universities even though most of them have retained their original names at the behest of the party-state. A notable exception is Southwest Normal University, which has changed its name to Southwest University.

2. *Mahjong* is a popular game in China. It is normally played by four persons. A full *Mahjong* set consists of 136 tiles. The game is a favorite pastime in Chinese communities but is considered to encourage the practice of gambling.

3. The "Puppet Manchukuo Regime ['Puppet Manchurian State']" was established by the Japanese military when it occupied the three northeastern provinces of China (Liaoning, Jilin, and Heilongjiang) during

1932–1945. China's last emperor Pu Yi was made head of state. Its capital was established in Changchun in the province of Jilin.

4. During the Cultural Revolution, the universities lost control of their own properties as various predatory groups commandeered or occupied their lands and buildings for a variety of purposes. Some of these properties were never returned to the educational institutions even after the return of normalcy.

5. In the early 1980s, the university admissions rate was approximately 4% of high school graduates who sat for the unified university entrance examinations.

6. The universities in China were administered under a dual-authority system where the presidents and the professors attended to academic affairs and the Party secretary and functionaries attended to student affairs. Student affairs were closely linked to the assurance of political rectitude and correct behaviors. The system was replaced by "revolutionary committees" during the Cultural Revolution when university administration was undermined. The dual-authority system was reinstated after the Cultural Revolution ended. For his first job, Teacher Yu worked as a student counselor in the Party stream of the newly reinstated dual-authority system.

7. The late Prof. Wang Fengxian was a prominent philosopher of education well known for his work in moral education. He is one of the "influential Chinese educators" featured in Hayhoe's (2007) book, *Portraits of influential Chinese educators*, which is discussed in the present study.

8. It is common for doctoral supervisors to choose the topics of theses for their students in China. This naturally raises the question of student autonomy. When the question of whether his own autonomy as a student was undermined, YW argued that the topic of his thesis on postmodernism, though assigned, did fit his own scholarly interest, and he did not mind the assignment. This Chinese tradition in doctoral supervision, when transported overseas, has puzzled many doctoral supervisors in Western societies where the choice of topics for doctoral research is respected as a domain of academic freedom. Rather than being students with no independent thinking, doctoral students from the Chinese Mainland may have their own ideas of scholarly pursuits, but, being observant of traditions, they may simply be waiting for encouragement from their supervisors to become more assertive in making their research interests known.

9. In other countries, the pressure on new faculty to demonstrate research productivity has caused difficulty for them to maintain their doctoral research interests as well. This phenomenon is apparent in the field of teacher education in the USA where the direction of reform has favored

a model of clinically rich teacher preparation. See, for example, Yendol-Hoppey et al. (2013).

10. This is in reference to Mao Zedong as the poet who launched the ambitious Great Leap Forward in 1958 with the purpose of elevating the development of China to a new height through indigenous means of industrial production. The campaign lasted for two years. Undermined by natural calamities and exaggerated production figures, the Great Leap Forward ended in disaster. Millions of people perished because of erroneous policies of the campaign. See, for example, Bachman (1991), MacFarquhar (1983), Perkins (1991).

11. The role of intellectuals in societal development has changed in the course of modern and contemporary Chinese history. In the late nineteenth century, they proposed ways to strengthen China against foreign encroachment. During the Republican period (1912–1949), they were the core impetus to reform endeavors that aimed to facilitate the country's early modernization experiments in the polity, society, economy, and education. The May Fourth Movement, which took place from 1919 onward, saw progressive Chinese intellectuals adopting the role of change agents who actively sought radical measures to change political participation, social relations, and educational thinking. The intellectuals remained as an important force in Chinese society and politics after the Communists came to power in 1949. With politics in a state of flux, their place in the society was made vulnerable by the oscillation of policies, which cast them in a position that vacillated between elation and despair. As China opened its door to the outside world in the 1980s, their advice was sought by the powers that be who wanted China to catch up with the industrialized countries and to play an active role in world affairs. Of late, the intellectuals' no longer enjoy their elevated status in national affairs as China, having secured its place among the world powers, has entered a new phase of development that saw a resurgence of emphases on political rectitude. See, for elaboration, Chow (1960), Wang (1966), Keenan (1977), Goldman and Lee (2002), Cheek (2015).

References

Bachman, D. (1991). *Bureaucracy, economy, and leadership in China: The institutional origins of the Great Leap Forward.* New York: Cambridge University Press.

Cheek, T. (2015). *The intellectual in modern Chinese history.* Cambridge: Cambridge University Press.

Chow, T. T. (1960). *The May Fourth Movement: Intellectual revolution in Modern China.* Cambridge, MA: Harvard University Press.

Goldman, M., & Lee, L. O. F. (Eds.). (2002). *An intellectual history of Modern China*. New York: Cambridge University Press.

Hayhoe, R. (2007). *Portraits of influential Chinese educators*. Dordrecht, Netherlands: Springer.

Keenan, B. (1977). *The Dewey experiment in China: Educational reform and political power in the early Republic*. Cambridge, MA: Harvard University Press.

MacFarquhar, R. (1983). *The origins of the Cultural Revolution* (Vol. 2). New York: Columbia University Press.

Perkins, D. (1991). China's economic policy and performance. In R. MacFarquhar, J. K. Fairbank, & Twitchett, D. (Eds.), *The Cambridge History of China* (Vol. 15, Chap. 6). Cambridge: Cambridge University Press.

Wang, Y. C. (1966). *Chinese intellectuals and the West, 1872–1949*. Chapel Hill, NC: University of North Carolina Press.

Yendol-Hoppey, D., Hoppey, D., Morewood, A., Hayes, S. B., & Graham, M. S. (2013). Micropolitical and identity challenges influencing new faculty participation in teacher education reform: When will we learn? *Teachers College Record, 115*(7), 1–31.

Yu, K. P. (2014). An essay on officialism (Guanben Zhuyi): A political analysis of Chinese Traditional Society. *Journal of Chinese Political Science, 19*(3), 235–247. doi:10.1007/s11366-014-9297-z.

Yu, W., & Qin, Y. Y. (2009). Bentu wenti yishi yu jiaoyu lilun bentuhua [Local issue awareness and the localization of educational theory]. *Jiaoyu Yanjiu* [*Educational Research*], 6, 27–31.

CHAPTER 3

Sifting Through the Enigma of Tradition and Modernity

Abstract As new ideas began to emerge with the growing openness of the country, the professor embraced them and used them to enrich his scholarship. For him, tradition, modernity, and postmodernity were not antithetical terms, for they constituted his knowledge base in ways that suited his development. Tradition expressed itself in different forms, from the artifacts of local cultures to a system of competitive examinations. He recognized of the grip of tradition on the country's development but believed that tradition has played a vital role in preserving the indigenous culture. He saw the ideas and practices of "class struggle" as a part of the revolutionary tradition. Yet, he loathed the cruelty which was displayed during the Cultural Revolution and the "banality of evil" that pervaded the society.

Keywords Tradition and modernity in education · Postmodernism and education · Cultural revolution · Open-door policy

Teacher Yu liked to quote from the Confucian classics, especially when he was dealing with issues of profound significance. From his selection of a motto for the Faculty of Education to his advocacy for an approach to "natural education," he was more than willing to tap the wisdom of traditional Chinese thought. Like many of his contemporaries, Teacher Yu benefitted from the openness of a historic period that saw the circulation of a growing array of social and political doctrines that traced

© The Author(s) 2018
F. Wang and L.N.K. Lo, *Navigating Educational Change in China*,
Curriculum Studies Worldwide, DOI 10.1007/978-3-319-63615-3_3

their intellectual origins to different historic, cultural, and ideological traditions. Chinese intellectuals could now gain access to the works of Western liberal thinkers, such as Kant, Rousseau, and Locke, in addition to the state-sanctioned works of socialist thinkers. Teacher Yu's interest in postmodernism called for the inclusion of the field's luminaries. Thus, the intellectual sources that constituted his epistemological foundation were a conflation of traditional and modern thinking. There was no clear and predictable demarcation between different types of ideas—traditional, modernist, or postmodernist—that he would employ in his social and educational observations. The perspectives which informed his observations were context-specific ideas that inspired him at the time. Consistently present in his observations, however, was the influence of history on his views on China's developmental endeavors, especially on its arduous modernization project. For Teacher Yu, the dialectics of tradition and modernity generated such a developmental puzzle that it should be appropriately examined under the lens of national and personal history. "You can't choose the age that you're born into and you can't choose history," he remarks, "Whether you like it or not, your life is closely linked to history and tradition" (Interview 4, 2014: 9).

The Grip of Tradition

China's search for the appropriate form and pace of development for its modernization project was punctuated by revolutions and wars that forced the abandonment of reform policies and programs that aimed to deliver the country from poverty and backwardness. For Chinese reformers who were engaged in this century-long project, one of the major reasons for its setbacks was the tenacity of tradition. When viewed as an antithesis of modernity, which emblematized the work of reformers, the tradition was considered the stranglehold that restricted societal progress. Tradition was presented, for example, as the embodiment of forces that impeded reform efforts in education and public health: Mass illiteracy was accepted as a historic fact; girls were deprived of schooling because of structural gender discrimination; and mass public health measures, such as preventive vaccination, were resisted because of widespread superstition. From this perspective, the grip of traditional norms and customs on the Chinese people has prevented the modernization project from taking root in the country.

For Teacher Yu, the grip of tradition could be viewed from multiple perspectives. Aside from the restrictions that it imposed on the modernization project, tradition—with its norms, customs, and lore—served to sustain cultural beliefs and practices that were vital for the preservation of the indigenous culture. These cultural beliefs were instilled, and practices were reinforced as historic inevitabilities that transcended the choice of the individual. He elaborates:

> If you were born in a certain province, you can't help that your taste in food and certain habits are linked to [that province]. I've said this before: your taste in food shows where you come from. [Your taste] was given to you by your parents. You don't have a choice. For example, it's often said that people from the Jiangsu Province like food that's sweet, or that people of the Shanxi [Province] like food that's sour. This [preference] was taught by your parents from birth … even if you discard this [taste] later, it's still in you, and flowing through your body. (Ibid.)

In considering the influence of tradition on their country's modernization endeavors, Chinese reformers placed emphasis on the systemic level. Their interests were in the injection of ideas, methods, and capital that could strengthen China's institutions so that they could help the country attain its developmental goals. Such goals were more than simply economic progress, as their achievement required the transformation of the whole society through the construction of modern institutional infrastructures. Thus, for the Chinese intellectuals and educators, the concept of "tradition" took on a deeper meaning than the simple signification of underdevelopment.

In the above light, "tradition" displays at least three characteristics which correspond with critical historical epochs that serve as contexts for their manifestation. The first form of tradition refers to the commonly understood structure of beliefs, thoughts, norms, customs, and habits which ferment patterns that influence people's thinking and behaviors through time.[1] For example, the long tradition of selecting state officials through the imperial examinations had been sustained for over a thousand years, and its influence is still being felt today. The second tradition is accredited to the intellectuals of the May Fourth Movement in the early twentieth century for the critical spirit that they instilled in a new sociopolitical outlook that was based on scientism and democracy. It was through this movement that Chinese intellectuals became actively involved in national affairs while serving as change agents for reform. For cultural renewal, the intellectuals called for democratic participation in the polity and society, scientific exploration of truth, and acceptance of modern values and practices. Through this tradition, the Chinese intellectuals came closest to realizing their "modernist" aspirations.[2] The third tradition, the "revolutionary tradition," was heralded by early revolutionaries of the Chinese Communist Party, including Mao Zedong, and flourished during the Cultural Revolution when seemingly endless struggles against "class enemies" were sustained by revolutionary zeal. By linking ideology with morality, this tradition upheld political rectitude as the prime criterion for assessing a person's potentiality and worth.[3]

As a scholar-teacher, Teacher Yu was understandably concerned about the dynamics that were generated from the interplay of the three traditions. It would be to his benefit that he could make sense of the place of these traditions in his own development as a scholar and in his professional work as an educator. From the time when he was a boy witnessing the ugly spectacles of human cruelty during the Cultural Revolution, through his tenure as an academic *cum* administrator with duties to uphold rules and regulations, to his work as a primary school principal trying to change the ethos of an elite establishment, Teacher Yu has become aware of the simultaneous presence of these traditions in his life and work. Rather than wrestling with the contradictions that existed among the traditions, he saw these traditions as historic and cultural givens that could be forged into an axiological and intellectual anchor for the nation's pursuits.

For Teacher Yu, "tradition" was something to be inherited and preserved, for it provided cultural meanings for our thinking and canons of appropriateness for our action. He explains:

> For the survival and development of humankind, one important [source of] wisdom is found in [the concept] of "degree [of appropriateness]"('*du*'). An example is eating. If we eat too much or too little, our health will suffer. But what does 'too much' or 'too little' mean? Human beings finally understand this after a long period of application. We Chinese conclude that, while eating, eighty percent full is appropriate. The same principle applies when we're doing things. Leave an appropriate margin for unforeseen circumstances. (Interview 4, 2014: 3)

Teacher Yu believes in the central place of traditional wisdom in China's development, not just for maintaining an equilibrium in the lives of its people but also for the progress of such a vital sector as education as well. He uses the educational thought of Mao Zedong as an example to illustrate the importance of inheriting and preserving traditional wisdom. He elaborates:

> For example, the guiding principles of [our] education have been to nurture people who are developed in all aspects; and nurture people who are active in socialist construction and who can become its successors. This includes unifying education with productive labor. These are all Mao's ideas, which were set [as policy] in 1957. We place emphasis on moral education today and claim that it should be our foremost concern. This was his advocacy in the 1940s. Of course, Mao inherited the educational tradition of China. Putting the nurturing of people, nurturing their moral rectitude, at the top [of the education agenda] is part of the Chinese educational tradition. (Interview 2 2014: 5)

Teacher Yu also advocates learning from and preserving traditional wisdom in educational inquiry, for he is concerned over "the absence of evidence of traditional heritage" in today's educational inquiry. He wants to go beyond the half-truths and myths that were bred by political hearsay so that he could achieve a full understanding of tradition in its real and original form. There is no dearth of topics related to the educational tradition in his research agenda. He allows: "I want to examine the imperial examinations, … and education in the Old Liberation Areas. My data collection is almost complete. I want to examine education during the Cultural Revolution, from the perspectives of education theory, of culture, of literature, and of film. I want to dig deep [into the issues]. We need to take a few steps back so that we can know where [today's] Chinese education is coming from" (Interview 1, 2009: 7).

The educational inquiry needs to be grounded in history and tradition so that new ideas for the future can be cultivated. Teacher Yu's adherence to this principle has led him to assert that: "Only when we remain faithful to the past can we hope to innovate" (Interview 4, 2014: 10). The past, however, could also be a cruel reminder of woeful events that brought out the worst of human nature. As the mayhem of the Cultural Revolution would attest, it is a part of the "tradition" too.

THE CULTURAL REVOLUTION AS TRADITION

One question that seems to have puzzled Teacher Yu is how the Cultural Revolution has come to epitomize the revolutionary tradition because of the calamities that it bred. When he was five years old, Teacher Yu witnessed the widespread disturbances that rained down on society. "Political struggle" rallies to denounce "class enemies," confrontations between factions of Red Guards, militia parades, horrific deaths of university students, and public mourning of those killed during the bloodshed were all a part of his life then. He recalls some of the frightful scenes:

> At the time, there were photos of dead people on display at the university. From the photos, you could see how they died. I could also see that some people were carrying long spears [on the campus]. The students made them. The spears were like those used in the ancient wars. The students even converted tractors into 'tanks', and I would climb on top them and fooled around. That left a strong impression. I can still see those fights. I remember there was a pile of discarded radiator panels that battling students would use as a shield against flying bullets. And I remember my grandmother telling me to get down, because the students, still fighting, were coming our way. (Interview 2, 2014: 10)

Aside from the scenes of the deadly conflicts, Teacher Yu also remembers a site near his home that was being called the "rebels building." It was there that the remains of the casualties of the armed strife were buried. Some floral wreaths were left there, and he learned for the first time that floral wreaths were for the dead (Ibid.). All these spectacles have left a powerful image on his psyche.

For Teacher Yu, the most perplexing aspect of the Cultural Revolution is how human nature was contorted into a grotesque display of hatred and fear. He asks: "How could classmates and even spouses turn against each other?" As if to accentuate the severity of his question, he laments with a recitation of a poem on sibling rivalry by Cao Zhi, a famous poet in the Han Dynasty: "All born of the same root; why are we inflicting this furious torment on each other?" (Ibid.: 11). To him, the Cultural Revolution "was a torturous inquisition into human nature, and a naked exposure of its dark side" (Ibid.). It was the ways that educated people humiliated, harmed, and even killed each other that perplexed him. Equally disturbing to Teacher Yu was the all-encompassing fear that enveloped the society. It was an era when the possession of knowledge was a common fear and blessed ignorance was the surest guarantee of one's safety. No one wanted to be identified as a learned person or a pursuer of knowledge. He observes: "The intellectuals didn't dare to study, and the students wouldn't study. Not studying was the honorable thing to do. [This is because] studying signified the road of the wayward professionals.[4] There were people who had to close the curtains when they wanted to study because they didn't want to be branded as successors of revisionism" (Interview 5, 2016: 6).

When he began serious exploration of educational issues, Teacher Yu wanted to choose the Cultural Revolution as the focal point of his inquiry because he wanted to understand the reason for the rampant cruelty that plagued human interaction, especially that which was evident in the relationships between the educated. He asks: "These people were school-mates, so how could they kill each other simply because of differences in beliefs? Why were they so cruel?" (Interview 3, 2014: 18–19). And, as if to offer a ready vindication for the incredible atrocities, he opines:

> Later, there was an explanation that we were fed wolf's milk and grew up on it. I think [this referred to] those decades of 'class [struggle] education'. It prepared a lot of people ideologically, which was, the way that we were supposed to confront our [class] enemies. We should be like the autumn winds sweeping fallen leaves. We should be cold and merciless like the severe winters. So the seeds were sown by seventeen years of 'class struggle education'. We knew how we could make sense of 'class struggle education'. In that way, apparently, education had had a role in some functions in [the Cultural Revolution]. I wonder if that made the younger people think that way. Was it through education? Was it through their teachers? We should use the ten years of the Cultural Revolution to reflect on education of the 'New China'.... What was in the seventeen years of pre-Cultural Revolution education that had led to emergence of the Red Guards? We need to find out more about this in order to understand the current state of affairs in Chinese education. (Ibid.: 19)

While the questions that Teacher Yu posed could be transformed into serious research questions, his plan to investigate the origins and consequences of education in the Cultural Revolution had to be delayed under the advice of his mentor. Because it was a very sensitive topic involving numerous actors and their legacies, the investigation may be postponed indefinitely under the long shadow cast by the Cultural Revolution. Interestingly, Teacher Yu never referred to the Cultural Revolution as an episode of the "revolutionary tradition." Nevertheless, it was clear that certain phenomena, such as "class struggle education" and the conspicuous absence of compassion in society, were evidential signifiers of that tradition. It troubled him that, during the Cultural Revolution, people seemed to have grown accustomed to the pervading sense of despair (Ibid.). As people's tolerance for cruelty, suffering, and depravity grew, evil became mundane and was accepted as an integral though loathsome part of human existence. Living with the "banality of evil" was an experience that was carved in the lives of those who suffered through the years of the Cultural Revolution.

"Banality of Evil" as a Fact of Life

Teacher Yu cited the works of Hannah Arendt when he referred to the "banality of evil." He talked admiringly about Arendt's insights into the sufferings of the Jewish people under Nazism. He says: "It's Arendt's ability to conceptualize that has attracted me. We've seen similar phenomena, but we haven't conceptualized them.... Her 'banality of evil' manages to bring out the nature of the phenomena in the most profound way" (Interview 3, 2014: 2). Teacher Yu agreed that the atrocities should not be blamed solely on Hitler as there were so many people who stood by and did nothing about them. Likewise, there were a lot of Chinese who stood by and did nothing to stop the barbarity of the Cultural Revolution. In trying to relate Arendt's concept of the "banality of evil" to the Chinese context, Teacher Yu infers: "She saw that there was a mass relinquishment of responsibilities. People were pushing [the responsibilities] out, [and said that] I don't know what to do about this. I'm powerless. If we let it go on, then evil will continue to exist for a long time" (Ibid.).

For Teacher Yu, the "banality of evil" has now taken on a new guise, lurking in the classrooms where teaching and learning are manipulated in the quest for higher test scores, and where teachers do not assume real responsibility for the authentic education of their students. He was not alone in connecting the "evil" of examination-oriented education to Arendt's concept, as such linkage has gained considerable attention among Chinese educators in the recent past (e.g., see Shi 2011). Teacher Yu saw the examination-oriented education that has undermined teaching and learning in China as a structural problem that was perpetuated by all stakeholders:

> Actually the examination in itself doesn't harm our students, or affect them adversely. [The problem] is that [its role] has been filtered through the lens of teachers and principals.... This includes the parents as well. That's why we have seldom treated [examination-oriented education] as something evil.... If one person does something evil, [we usually see] it as a problem caused by an individual; but if so many people are doing the same [evil] thing, then it is a problem of the system and policies. (Ibid.: 3)

For the perpetuation of the examination-oriented tradition in Chinese education, Teacher Yu faults the teachers for their reluctance and inability to assert their professionalism. He says:

> From what I've seen so far, I think very few teachers engage in independent thinking. Most of the teachers don't. They just follow what the school principals tell them. Or they will follow the traditions of the schools, and the course syllabi. [Because] they don't have their own thinking, our teachers prefer to obey and they like being told what to do. They'll do whatever is needed to make the students get higher test scores. One consequence of this kind of behavior is that [the teachers end up] not taking any responsibility. They push their responsibilities outward. They think that they're helpless and are just following what the school principal tell them to do. So it becomes other people's responsibility.... But what if the principals are wrong? The absence of reflection and independent thinking among our teachers is a reason for the 'banality of evil' to exist in Chinese education. A lot of people consider that thinking independently involves risk-taking; and to conform is the safest things to do. This is a problem in Chinese education that deserves our utmost attention. (Interview 2, 2014: 15)

On the tradition of the examination-oriented education, Teacher Yu chooses to focus his observation on the social conditions of the Chinese people. He explains:

> The living conditions of a lot of our people have yet to surpass the level of survival. For a lot of families, the survival of their children is a major issue because of all the uncertainties and insecurities in their lives. They have to grasp the [opportunity offered by] university entrance examination as if it is the straw that can save them. It is much better than living your life by relying on the good grace of others and on social connections. This

is especially true for those people who lack social capital and connections, those who don't have any money, any power. What are they going to do? The only thing they can do is to swallow the bitterness and work as hard as they can, as long as they don't die. This is why educational reform in China is so difficult. We need to consider these conditions a reality in our nation. (Interview 3, 2014: 5)

For many Chinese, particularly those living in the countryside, doing well in the examinations and getting admitted into the universities provide an avenue of hope, a way out of the backwardness and poverty of rural life. This sense of hope explains why Chinese parents would make sacrifices—"dismantle their stoves to sell cast iron" (in Teacher Yu's words)—in order to support the schooling of their children. The consequence of this single-minded pursuit is an extremely low tolerance for change that is brought on by educational reform. Teacher Yu remarks: "Reform is not given the slightest margin of error. For if you're wrong, it will ruin my child's life. Then I'll have to ruin your life" (Ibid.: 6).

Teacher Yu is more critical when he tries to explain the acquiescence of teachers and the examination-oriented tradition in Chinese education. He takes the stance of an educator who is cognizant of the inherent injustice of the education system and the teachers' inability to effect changes to the structure of schooling. As he searches for the impediments to progress in educational reform during the last decade, it becomes clear that the forces of tradition have rendered him and other educators as powerless as the masses. He refers to the ancient Chinese tradition of "those who study well should become officials" (*xueeryiu zeshi*), and reiterates the central role of the examinations. He asks: "Why is schooling so important?," and then replies: "Because it's beneficial. Perhaps it is beneficial to one's thinking, or beneficial to one's occupation, to one's life, or to whatever" (Ibid.: 4).

For Teacher Yu, the tenacity of the examination-oriented tradition reflects its intimate linkage to the survival of the people. Perhaps it is success in examination, the ultimate test of the outcome of schooling, which has become the most direct way for the offspring of ordinary folks to elevate themselves socially and to rise above the level of survival. In traditional China, the surest way to do this was to become an official who was given the power to control human and material resources. Teacher Yu has referred to the plight of "officialism" that has permeated Chinese society for centuries and is still evident today (e.g., Yu 2014). Yet, as an intellectual who has held out for an "academic democracy" in which scholars would be recognized for their intellectual prowess rather than their official positions, he thinks that "China still has a long way to go" (Interview 2, 2014: 10). As he reflects on his own role as an intellectual, Teacher Yu seems acutely aware of his own powerlessness in altering the *status quo*. He admits: "At present, you can't expect to change reality simply by writing essays. That's the false pretension of the ancient sages" (Interview 3, 2014: 13).

Teacher Yu's realization of the limits of his own capacity as an intellectual and an educator was prompted by an encounter with a couple of shepherd girls during one of his field trips to the Qinghai Autonomous Region in 2006. Qinghai was a poor area in the western part of the country where the central government was keen to implement free and compulsory education. At the time, Teacher Yu was serving as a member of an "expert group" convened to inspect the state of implementation of compulsory education in the region. The two girls were around ten years of age. They were walking with a donkey on a hill, but not attending school. Teacher Yu asked them: "Why aren't you in school? It's free." One of the girls answered: "Yes it's free. But if we go to school we wouldn't be able to make money. This is a tourist area, and if I walk around with my donkey [and allow people to take pictures with me], I'll make 30 yuan (approximately US$ 5). We need to have our dowry ready when we get to be fourteen and then get married by sixteen." Later, Teacher Yu confesses: "If I weren't there, I wouldn't have been able to truly understand the difficulty of implementing compulsory education in China. This is because it involved a lot of issues related to local customs and how they have affected people's view on education" (Interview 2, 2014: 6).

HISTORY, MODERNITY, AND POSTMODERNITY

Teacher Yu's views on modernity are closely linked to his understanding of tradition. Such views represent an interesting mixture of historical realism and developmental pragmatism. From his observation on the cultural and educational renewal of China and its possible way out of developmental dilemmas, Teacher Yu often refers to the lessons of history and attempts to tap its wisdom. He supports his insistence on the essentiality of history in educational research by arguing that education has a historical mission of perpetuating the Chinese culture. He explains:

One characteristic of education as a field of inquiry is that it has to deal with the same kinds of problems that human beings have faced before. Or the problems may be similar. So we have to go back in time and explore the origins of these problems. For example, what is human nature? What is education? What is morality? We would have to go back to the times of Confucius, Lao Zi, or even Socrates to find a perspective [to approach the problems]. So when we say we're proposing a so-called 'new idea' or a 'new concept', we have to review history to find out who has thought about such matters before, and how they were being approached. At least one should know that our predecessors have dealt with them. Or else we'll be thinking mistakenly that we're creating something new, while others had actually created the same [concept] a hundred years ago. This is why I pay a lot of attention to history. (Interview 3, 2014: 4)

Teacher Yu's allegiance to history is not confined to educational inquiry alone, for he is convinced that history can serve as an epistemological anchor for our understanding of society and culture. From the life history of his cousin Dongming, who was forced out a job that could make good use of his talents because of his "undesirable political background," to the experiences of noteworthy scholars who were purged during politically radical times, "history provided a valuable context for exploration and understanding" (Ibid.: 8). Teacher Yu thinks that history should also be central to the study of a modernizing society like China, for without an understanding of the historical forces that have shaped its development, there could be no basis for further exploration of the modern, which is in fact an extension of history.

Teacher Yu is pragmatic in his observation on modernity and things modern. For example, he has not mentioned, as the Chinese reformers in the late Qing Dynasty and Republican period had done, the promises of modernization in material terms, such as the rapid industrialization that could generate wealth and power for the nation. Instead, he chooses to focus on the kinds of change that modernity can bring to people's thinking and worldview. He agrees partially with the reformers of old that China's modernization endeavor, a project of human transformation, should rely on reason as its basis of judgment, science should be the instrument for truth-seeking, and secularization should be a process of liberating human potentials from supernatural constraints (Yu 2005: 51–52). Emerging from this modernist outlook is an educational vision that casts its aim to the future: Education should be about the nurturing of people for the future. The modernist educational vision establishes science at the center of educational inquiry, curriculum design, and the pedagogy. In the classroom, teaching and learning will reflect the increased systemization and differentiation of knowledge. The pedagogical process will rely on the ability of teachers to instruct and to guide while they serve as "spokespersons for science, reason, and truth" (Ibid.: 52). Given the fact that Teacher Yu has expressed reservations about the dominance of scientism in Chinese education, there is some evidence that his endorsement of the aforesaid modernist approach is mixed with certain skepticism regarding its unbridled influence in the educational reality of China.

Teacher Yu's most acute observation on modernity is found in his analysis of "modernity" in relation to "postmodernity," an area of study in which he has devoted considerable time and attention. He notes that aside from its faith in positivist science as the real truth-seeker, modernity also places emphasis on reason, individuality, and the power of human intervention to create and change one's own existence. He sees modernity as a process of rationalization that leads Chinese thinking toward "abstract reduction, qualitative computation, accurate prediction, and efficient control" (Ibid.: 51). For him, postmodernist thinking presents a challenge to the legitimacy of the modernist views on human progress by reacting against the injustices that are created by such a rationalization process (Ibid.: 53). "Postmodernity," being a condition associated with changes in society and institutions, delineates problems in the application of principles of rationality and hierarchy to public life. Postmodernists object to the structural violence that modern institutions level against the marginalized and disadvantaged groups in society and demand that diversity and differences be recognized in society and education. "Postmodernism lets us pay attention to those sectors that have been marginalized for a long time" (Interview 3, 2014: 9). He reflects:

The spread of postmodernist thinking allows us to have an expanded view of things, like things regional, local, and indigenous. In the past, we talked about knowledge that could be generalized, that was eternal, balanced, and applicable all over the world. Postmodernism advocates [an examination of] differences. So our research in educational psychology emphasizes 'school-based', [while other areas of inquiry stress] school-based curriculum development and school-based research. These [phenomena] are all related to the spread of postmodernist thinking. Thus we need to address the kind of problems that postmodernism has delineated. We can't totally nullify science and rationality; and we can't totally ignore the subjectivity of human beings. (Ibid.)

Teacher Yu observed that modernity and postmodernity are "twin brothers" because they shared a common concern in understanding and articulating "the modern." "In whatever ways that they have disagreed and argued, they will enrich each other in the end" (Yu 2005: 54).

Debates on the limitations of the modernist approach to education have been staged in Chinese education circles in recent years. According to Teacher Yu, some of the measures adopted for curriculum reform in China, an ongoing project that has lasted for decades, could be traced back to ideas that recognized salient problems in the modernist approach to education. In the main, these ideas advocate: resistance to the hegemony of positivist science in educational inquiry; appreciation of the construction and contextualization of knowledge and the essentiality of lived experience and emotion in teaching and learning; and alteration of the teacher's role from an authoritarian instructor to a caring facilitator for the students' pursuits in life (Ibid.: 53). While some of these ideas, as a reaction against the modernist approach to education, have been transformed into reform measures for application in the school context, Teacher Yu is not convinced that authentic modernist education has actually taken root in the education system. This was because "modernity," as we knew it, has yet to be accepted as an integral part of life in the Chinese society. He argues: "Our mainstream thinking is still reliant on experience rather than on rationality; and in social relations, emotional attachment is more important than law and contract. Rationality, liberty, science and individuality have not yet taken root in our society, but are in a state of 'rootless' drifting" (Ibid.: 54).

If Chinese society and education have yet to reach the stage of modernity, as Teacher Yu has claimed, then what relevance does the debate on modernity and postmodernity have for the educational development of China? (Interview 2, 2014: 2–3). Aside from his belief that the study of postmodernism could shed light on the necessity of addressing differences and diversity in Chinese society and education, Teacher Yu's confidence in the relevance of the debate is actually based on an assumption that certain aspects of development in Western societies today would become harbingers to the future development of China. For Teacher Yu, this assumption should justify an intellectual openness toward the learning of Western ideas and practices (Interview 3, 2014: 13). His vision of the role of Western ideas in China's development reflects a state of confusion that Chinese intellectuals and educators have shared while attempting to demarcate between tradition and modernity, and between

Western and Chinese. Through more than a century of experimentation, Chinese education has become an amalgam of traditional and modern (and even postmodern) traits (Interview 2, 2014: 4). Given China's increasing interaction with Western societies, it has become even more difficult to distinguish the modern from the Western. For China's current nation-building efforts, and for intellectual understanding, Teacher Yu thinks that it was more than necessary to examine the influence that Western values and ideas have had on his society so that a clearer sense of national identity can be attained.

Notes

1. See, for example, the two volumes of relevant materials compiled by William T. De Bary and his colleagues in De Bary and Bloom (1999), and De Bary and Lufrano (2000).
2. See, for example, Chow (1960), Grieder (1970), and Spence (1981).
3. For depictions of the influence of the revolutionary tradition on education, see Chen (1974), Hu (1974), and Seybolt (1973).
4. This is an approximate translation of the original term that Teacher Yu used during the interviews, "Baizhuan luxian," which should be translated literally as "White professional road." The term was used during periods of radical politics to depict those who focused on their own scholarly inquiry without paying adequate attention to learning from the teachings of Chairman Mao. Later, the term took on a broader meaning to include those who are devoted to their professional pursuits but demonstrate little interest in politics.

References

Chen, T. H. E. (1974). *The Maoist educational revolution.* New York: Praeger.

Chow, T. T. (1960). *The May Fourth Movement: Intellectual revolution in Modern China.* Cambridge, MA: Harvard University Press.

De Bary, W. T., & Bloom, I. (Eds.). (1999). *Sources of Chinese Tradition, vol. 1: From earliest times to 1600* (2nd ed.). New York: Columbia University Press.

De Bary, W. T., & Lufrano, R. (Eds.). (2000). *Sources of Chinese Tradition, vol. 2: From 1600 through the twentieth century* (2nd ed.). New York: Columbia University Press.

Grieder, J. B. (1970). *Hu Shih and the Chinese Renaissance: Liberalism in the Chinese revolution, 1917–1937.* Cambridge, MA: Harvard University Press.

Hu, C. T. (Ed.). (1974). *Chinese education under Communism.* New York: Teachers College Press.

Seybolt, P. J. (Ed.). (1973). *Revolutionary education in China: Documents and commentary*. White Plains, NY: M.E. Sharpe.

Shi, M. (2011). *Jiaoshe de pingyong zhiguo shi shenme* [What are the faults of teacher mediocrity?]. *Jiaoshe Bolan* [*Teacher Exposition*], December 2011. Retrieved from 21ccom.net on May 15, 2015.

Spence, J. D. (1981). *The gate of heavenly peace: The Chinese and their revolution, 1895–1980*. New York: Viking Press.

Yu, W. (2005). *Jiaoyuguan de xiandaixing weiji yu xinlujing chutan* [Modernity crisis of educational perspectives and research on the new route]. *Jiaoyu Yanjiu* [*Educational Research*], (3), 51–57.

Yu, K. P. (2014). An essay on officialism (Guanben Zhuyi): A political analysis of Chinese Traditional Society. *Journal of Chinese Political Science, 19*(3), 235–247. doi:10.1007/s11366-014-9297-z.

CHAPTER 4

Balancing the Indigenous and the Foreign

Abstract The professor celebrated the spirit of openness of the 1980s that allowed Chinese society to appreciate the concept of "I" and individuality. Acceptance of the centrality of the individual has empowered people to embrace choice and assume responsibility. However, the importation of Western ideas and practices has created tensions in education and society. They challenged Chinese educators to re-examine their instrumental approach to education and to address such issues as equality and diversity. In trying to resolve the tensions between Chinese and Western ideas and practices, the professor stressed the importance of illuminating Chinese characteristics in educational and cultural matters and proposed an integrative approach which would incorporate Western thinking and techniques into China's developmental agenda.

Keywords Western educational approach · Individuality and freedom Diversity and uniformity in education · Educational reform in china

China's relations with the Western world have been fluid and at times contentious. They have been strained by a century of wars, invasions, and failed ventures in cooperation for mutual benefits. Western ideas and practices have been tested, adopted, or rejected, depending on the political atmosphere of the times. Likewise, their fate in Chinese education has also mirrored an uncertain passage of tentative borrowing, leaving room for trials and experimentation. There has been no period

© The Author(s) 2018   69
F. Wang and L.N.K. Lo, *Navigating Educational Change in China*,
Curriculum Studies Worldwide, DOI 10.1007/978-3-319-63615-3_4

in contemporary Chinese history that foreign, especially Western, educational ideas and practices have circulated among Chinese universities and schools more prevalently than in the last three decades. During this period, foreign influence has been discernible in curriculum reform and pedagogical change, and in the approach to educational research and institutional building. For people in the education system, however, the treatment of matters foreign and indigenous has been a perpetual balancing act.

Teacher Yu credits Western ideas for illuminating the centrality of the individual in human existence and for enriching Chinese education. This has led to the affirmation of human agency and the needs for diversity in current educational reform endeavors. He looks back almost with affection to the decade of the 1980s when Chinese intellectuals and society were reacquainted with Western ideas that made their way into China through the "open doors," which symbolized a national policy that ended decades of isolation. It was an exciting time for Teacher Yu, for he could partake in the convivial spirit that celebrated openness and the discovery of new ideas. He recalls:

> The 1980s were one of the most liberated times in Chinese history. The gates of the nation were suddenly thrown open, Western thoughts were pouring in.... It was an age of enlightenment, an age of reflection for the Chinese people, on the Cultural Revolution, on the road that China had traveled, and on Chinese tradition. So there was a cultural upsurge, and we asked how we should look upon the culture of our ancestors, how we should treat feudalism, Western culture, the Yellow Earth [of our nation], and the sky-blue color [of the ocean that represented the West]. (Interview 3, 2014: 20)

Prominent intellectuals re-emerged to illuminate the cultural and literary scenes. Debates in university salons stirred the mind and enlivened the spirit. Streams of translated texts published by non-governmental agencies began to appear (Interview 4, 2014: 8). They introduced the works of Freud, Nietzsche, and Existentialism to young people who had never heard of them before. The publication of translated texts by civil organizations rather than government publishers was a significant phenomenon in itself. In this, Teacher Yu discerns an epochal change. He says:

From 1949 to 1979, for thirty years, the translations of a lot of Western works was organized or commissioned by the government. [Publishing by civil organizations such as academic associations] was a change, from the top-down approach of the past to the bottom-up approach of the present. I can even say that the translation of certain Western works during the Cultural Revolution was the result of Chairman Mao's written comments on official documents [submitted] from below. When Chairman Mao said he wanted to read certain works by Marx, it meant that we could read some works by Kant and Hegel. If the Chairman didn't say anything, we couldn't read anything [Western]. That was a huge change. (Ibid.: 8–9)

Such a change was only the tip of an iceberg. "From the 1980s onward," Teacher Yu reminisces, "China began to stress democracy and the rule of law, the blooming of a hundred flowers. It was important for people to remain cool-headed. The 1980s was like an age of enlightenment. People called for humanism, for democracy and the rule of law, and for learning from abroad. And they could view all the inventions of human civilization peacefully and constructively.... There were real intellectual debates, a kind of dialogue that was based on equality, and not on the charity of any one Party" (Ibid.: 8).

Teacher Yu observes that the most important for the intellectuals was the re-institution of university entrance examinations, a systemic mechanism that had perpetuated China's "meritocratic system" for over a millennium. In the 1980s, the examinations allowed the most academically prepared students to gain entrance into higher institutions. As one of the early beneficiaries of the re-institution policy, Teacher Yu was admitted into the university in 1981 and seemed to be proud of his accomplishment in the fiercely competitive exercise that admitted only 4% of applicants (Interview 3, 2014: 20). He says:

It was when the society was transforming. Let me put it this way: it was a good time for university students to find a spouse. Back then, public recognition of a university student was even higher than that of a doctoral student today. People wanted to learn, tried to get into the universities, and studied. It was considered a noble thing. A kind of atmosphere took shape. People wanted to read books. They strived to read as much as they could. There was no distraction, because there was no Internet then. There were just books printed on paper; and there were so few books. People strived to be the first to read them. (Ibid.)

Equally impressive was the fact that the re-instituted university entrance examinations "seemed to have congregated these enthusiastic pursuers of knowledge in the higher institutions and research institutes in one fell swoop" (Ibid.). They were passionately engaged in their study, as if to make up for lost time. Some of them believed that the urgent task at hand was the popularization of new knowledge and skills, including those that were freshly imported from the West. It would be through the injection of new ideas and practices that the society and education of China could be rejuvenated. One of the consequences of importing Western ideas and knowledge was their swift inclusion in the Chinese vocabulary of that period. Teacher Yu likes to enumerate some of these Western concepts, some of which were imported and gained popularity during the 1980s: "Independent thinking, self-actualization, rationalization, subjectivity, humanism and alienation.... These keywords keep pouring out [from my mind]. They keep pouring out" (Ibid.: 21).

The Discovery of "I" and Individuality

Among the imported "core concepts" from the West, Teacher Yu considers the recognition of the centrality of the individual in human existence to be the most important. He speculates that it was the influx of Western knowledge and values during the 1980s that had fostered an awareness of the concept of the individual in the society. The word "I" was seldom used in the past, but through the popularization of translations of Western literature and the rise of new indigenous literary groups, the concept of "I" began to gain currency among university students. It was used to denote a person's existence, her subjective views on others, and her personal feelings. He reflects: "This was when you could talk about your loneliness. It was taboo to talk about 'I' in revolutionary times, and surely you could not talk about your personal sufferings ... because you belonged to the organization. You didn't belong to yourself" (Interview 2, 2014: 22).

The emergence of "I" in the contemporary cultural narrative brought relief to a people who were used to identifying with "we," as "we" in the family, in the work-unit, and in the nation. In a sense, the market economy that was born in the 1980s affirmed the centrality of "I," the individual, in societal development. In liberating the energy of the masses by giving them the opportunities to choose their own pursuits, the market economy actually placed the burden of making the right choice on the person. Teacher Yu explains:

> Before that, you didn't have to be responsible for yourself, because the Party, the country, and your parents were all responsible for you. When people started having freedom in the 1980s, and with the unified job assignment system gone, you've got to think for yourself. Previously, thinking for yourself was useless. You were supposed to be a brick in the Party's wall, something that the Party could move around at will. (Ibid.)

With the newly found freedom to develop, "you were responsible for what you did, it was your choice, and that was the kind of objective condition [that the market economy had provided] for our conversion from 'we' to 'I'" (Interview 2, 2014: 1).

Recognition of the centrality of the individual has empowered people to assume responsibility and to think and live their lives in ways that they have chosen for themselves. Because of this development, people began to base their decisions on reason rather than on faith—faith that was based on the singularity of ideology that traced its origin back to the thoughts of Marx and Mao Zedong. "In the past," Teacher Yu observes, "we in China listened to those whom we worshipped, and we were told that we could only listen to those persons.... You're allowed to think now, and that's a significant change" (Ibid.: 11).

Education was one of the most significant areas to be changed by the injection of Western ideas in the increasingly complex societal context. The uniform approach to education, and its singular path to mobility and success, appeared ineffective as it failed to inspire the intellect of the young and to invigorate their passion. The singular path led too many students to the "narrow log bridge" where they had to compete with each other in examinations in order to reach the gates of the nation's universities. "The Chinese people have only one path, one root," Teacher Yu says, "I'm sure that people in other countries weren't like us, with so many people wanting to get into Beijing University. I don't think there would be so many Americans wanting to get into Harvard" (Interview 4, 2014: 11).

He is particularly concerned over the uniform approach of the Chinese pedagogy which paled against the potpourri of Western approaches and methods that aimed to engage students in learning. He admits: "In China, we like things to be orderly and uniform, we like [our students] to be the same: walk the same way, sit the same way. The lesson plans are all the same, the mode of teaching is the same" (Interview 3, 2014: 25). Looking back into history, Teacher Yu attributes this inclination to uniformity to the ways that social programs had been initiated in the past: "The development of China has been driven by social campaigns, by administrative orders, so that [it could be achieved] in an orderly and uniformed manner.... We used to advocate one kind of thinking, one outlook, one way of life. We have multiple perspectives now" (Interview 4, 2014: 8). As if to remind himself that this phenomenon would not just be a fleeting episode, he draws reassurance by reciting from an ancient text: "Things are created in harmony; it is uniformity that impedes their development"[1] (*Zheng Yu in Guo Yu*, n. d.).

The Utilization of Western Ideas and Practices

Teacher Yu views the importation of Western educational ideas and practices with guarded optimism, for they challenge the Chinese people to re-examine their instrumental approach to education: to view education as an avenue to power and wealth; to obtain tangible benefits from success in examinations; to seek special privileges by gaining admission into elite institutions; and "to accomplish these objectives once and for all so that one's life can be secured forever" (Interview 4, 2014: 10). He elaborates:

> The Chinese people have put too much emphasis on fame and fortune. Western educational thinking could help to reduce the influence of some of the educational views we inherited from the past. For example, such sayings as 'In the books one can find ladies as fair as jade and houses of gold' and 'To be a scholar is the noblest of all human pursuits' have great influence on the ordinary people. That's why 'marks' [given in examinations] have always occupied such an important position in the Chinese mind. [The Chinese] have to study, get high marks, and go to good schools. That's why vocational education has never flourished in China. China is a society of credentialism. Competition in the university entrance exam is so keen. [Our universities] are admitting so many more people, and yet the competitive environment is still brutal. I think this [phenomenon] has a lot to do with 'social insurance' lagging behind social development, and with parental expectations and the effects of traditional norms. People want to 'strive to accomplish something desirable once and for all'. They want to get into Beijing University then everything will be fine. Actually they really

want to seek special privileges, to get a special pass, and then use it at their own pleasure. One can use it while loafing, use it without having to go to work, use it when one is eighty years old. I think this is a very important thing in the hearts of many Chinese. (Ibid.)

Teacher Yu thinks that the instrumentalist thinking in Chinese education is intimately linked to the social factor of "face," which affects the way that Chinese parents view the purpose of education. He uses the example of streaming students in schools to illustrate how parental preservation of "face" has affected the quality of education for the students:

[Streaming students in accordance with their academic performance] may perhaps work in other countries. But it is difficult to implement in China. Why is it difficult? Well, even if my child has the worst performance, I'd still want him to be in the best class. Or else I would lose face. This shows that face is more important than facts. I'd rather hold on to the delusive "face", which is considered to be more important than reality. Some principals have told me that streaming is very difficult, although it makes sense to stream students according to ability. But whenever they tried to divide students into different groups, someone would complain to the authorities.... Some parents try to get their children into the best schools, even though that may entail [their children] spending hours on the road.... That's why we now have large numbers of 'good school-districts apartments". The rents of apartments located near the famous schools are exceptionally high.... We in China view 'face' as the most important thing. It is a fact in the reality of the Chinese nation. If you want to do things the foreign way in China, it will be difficult. (Interview 3, 2014: 6)

Despite his reservations, Teacher Yu values certain aspects of Western educational thinking that may help to inform the developmental course of Chinese education by pointing to alternative ways of educating. To him, Western education gives children "freedom and flexibility [to explore]. It emphasizes choice and multiple approaches to educating. These are some of the things that we could learn from it" (Interview 5, 2016: 6). However, the "freedom and flexibility [afforded by Western education] may not ensure that 'all' children will become successful; but it might nurture geniuses" (Ibid.). Because of its emphasis on the development of the individual, Western education pays more attention to the developmental psychology of children (Interview 4, 2014: 12) and to accommodating their diverse learning needs. Certain Western educational ideas, some of which can be attributed to the progressive tradition of education in the West, have been incorporated into the blueprints for curriculum reform since the advent of the new century. Such reform efforts have brought changes in "the educational thinking of teachers, in the outlook of teaching and learning in the classroom, and in educational assessment in schools" (Interview 5, 2016: 6).

Teacher Yu sees the deployment of Western ideas and practices as instruments of change and a challenge to existing practices in Chinese education, which is being devitalized by social conformity and professional complacencies. However, despite his acceptance of the role that Western ideas and practices could play in China's educational reform, he has never endorsed them as a replacement for Chinese values in education. For Teacher Yu, they should merely be seen as something useful, like a mirror that could help the Chinese to reflect on the strengths and limitations of their own education system.[2] Like many of his predecessors who attempted to reform Chinese education by consulting Western experiences, Teacher Yu warns against "foreign worship." "This would only weaken our awareness of indigenous problems or even retard the growth of such an awareness," he writes (Yu and Qin 2009: 28). "[In China] where the indigenous knowledge base for modern education is weak, learning indiscriminately from the West may lead its education astray and even cause it to lose sight of the real problems at hand" (Ibid.).

In the twilight of the Qing Dynasty during the nineteenth century, Chinese reformers had advised that indigenous and Western knowledge should be differentiated in terms of the purpose and utility of each. The division between indigenous and Western knowledge by specific role in the design of developmental strategies seemed logical, since the intention of the reformers was to prevent the colonization of the Chinese culture (the indigenous) by Western values (the foreign). Through time, the principle proposed by a scholar-official, Zhang Zhidong—"Chinese scholarship as core, Western knowledge for application" (*zhongxue weiti xixue weiyong*)—has been widely used to differentiate the roles of indigenous and Western knowledge.[3] According to Zhang's principle, indigenous Chinese knowledge provided the "substance" of development, which included its purpose, rationale, and goals, while imported Western knowledge was to be used for its "function," which included methods of operation and tools. The acceptance of Western knowledge began with the recognition of its utility for inventing material goods, such as weaponry and machinery, which was then expanded to include some of the associated values, such as efficiency and quality.

For Teacher Yu, the recognition of the "substance" as well as the "function" of Western knowledge in education requires a gradual process that would be based on changes in the values and structure of Chinese education. He admits that "the modernization of education in developing countries is a process of Westernization in certain ways" (Ibid.), but he also argues that China should not limit its source of enlightenment and inspiration to Western knowledge. He writes: "As globalization deepens, and developing countries are gradually strengthening their interaction with countries from around the world, they no longer learn from a single country but seek to learn from many other countries" (Ibid.). In his argument, Teacher Yu identifies China as a "developing country" where educational development will be enhanced through the incorporation of good practices imported from a growing number of education systems around the world (Ibid.).

In Chinese education, the treatment of indigenous and foreign knowledge (including Western knowledge) has often been a point of contention, which oscillated between prevailing ideological beliefs and political conditions. On the balance between indigenous and Western knowledge, Teacher Yu opines that the indigenous context of Chinese education should provide the epistemological basis for the conversion of knowledge and values. He suggests a process that involves "modification, transformation, and creation." In such a process, imported ideas and practices would first be modified with reference to the indigenous context. They would then be changed to suit their in-context purposes and functions with sufficient space for the new ideas and practices to take hold (Interview 4, 2014: 12). To facilitate an effective conversion process, the imported Western knowledge would have to be understood correctly and thoroughly.

Because of his vocation, Teacher Yu is in a good position to pursue the kind of understanding that will facilitate the conversion exercise that he has suggested. His scholarly interest in modernity and postmodernity, as well as his role as a teacher, has given him opportunities to read, write, and reflect on Western ideas and practices from the perspective of educational philosophy. He has selected readings that could strengthen his own understanding of Western thought, especially those that were relevant to his scholarly pursuit: Kant, Rousseau, Locke, Marx, Weber, Dewey, and Arendt, and the masters of postmodernism, Lyotard,

Derrida, and Foucault, with convergent interests developed for the works of Bourdieu and Giddens (Interviews 2, 3, 4 *op. cit.*). He has led a project that translated the major works of Foucault into the Chinese language, and supervised student theses on Western thinkers and the treatment of their ideas in China, such as the popularization of Jerome Bruner's *The Process of Education* (Interview 2, 2014: 4).

Teacher Yu states that he has read William Pinar's *Understanding Curriculum* thrice (Ibid.: 3), for he was moved by that author's ability to anchor a broad range of issues in the person. Unlike Chinese academic writings "which merely present cold reasoning," he asserts, "there are feelings in [Pinar's work]" (Interview 3, 2014: 8). He was inspired by Pinar's methodological conception of "Currere"—the infinitive form of curriculum, which can be expressed in an educator's autobiographical reflection of life experiences (Pinar 1975). He initiated projects that attempted to link the history of academic disciplines to the lived experiences of prominent scholars (Interview 3, 2014: 8). For example, his biographical study on Chen Yuanhui, an educator, and his edited work on Huang Ji, a philosopher, are undertakings that connect their lived experiences to their ideas and work. Teacher Yu attributes this kind of inquiry to Pinar's influence on his work. He also thinks that the study of postmodernist theories has broadened his understanding of scholarly inquiry. He says: "Our understanding of the world shouldn't be limited to the quantifiable and the objective. There should be subjectivity in there as well" (Ibid.: 9).

The Western "theoretical resources" that have enabled Teacher Yu to explore new ways of inquiry (Interview 2, 2014: 11–13) have been buttressed by a knowledge base of Chinese scholarship that spans thinking from the ancient Chinese classics of Confucianism and Daoism to the writings of modern and contemporary Chinese thinkers such as Lu Xun, Mao Zedong, Li Zehou, Ge Zhaoguang, and Zhao Tingyang. It is from a Chinese theoretical perspective, a composite of classical and contemporary views on society and education, that Teacher Yu formulates his educational outlook. Western ideas and theories are used as a supplement to deepen understanding (such as using Arendt to elucidate the "banality of evil" during the Cultural Revolution) and to critique the *status quo* (using Foucault to illustrate structural violence against the individual). At the core of his concerns, however, are developmental issues that transcend national boundaries: development of humanism, environmental sustainability, social equity, peaceful coexistence, psychological well-being, technological advancement, and survival in the "digital age" (Interview 2, 2014: 11–14 *passim*).

Teacher Yu takes a pragmatic approach to addressing the aforementioned issues and views them in a Chinese context. He believes in the power of policies and institutions in solving these societal problems. He says: "we cannot merely rely on the self-cultivation of the individual" (Ibid., 13). Yet, he also believes in the efficacy of education in improving human character and people's living conditions (Ibid.). In the age of globalization when China's national strengths are being constantly tested in international affairs, "education is an integral part of national security and public affairs of the society" (Yu 2005: 54). He asserts:

If we want to bolster the composite strengths of our nation, then we must [develop] science and technology and [pay attention to] modernization; we must [cultivate] national consciousness and citizenship education; and we must rely on reason. Because of these [requirements], education in our nation, especially basic education, will necessarily embody values and practices that are instrumental, survivalist, and pragmatic. This determines the developmental direction and guiding ideology of our country's education, which has remained modernist. The only difference is that tints of diversity and differences have been applied to it. (Ibid.)

"CHINESE AURA"

Teacher Yu's pragmatic views on education's role in national development stem from a modernist perspective that sees education as an indispensable project that is a catalyst in the country's irresistible march toward modernity (Ibid.). In order to facilitate the accomplishment of that goal, he thinks that educational development should be imbedded in the culture and history of China, and should be able to convey a "Chinese Aura" (*Zhongguo qipai*) in its manifestations.[4] Unlike some of his compatriots who view the "Chinese Aura" phenomenon through the lens of national pride, such as China's impressive economic growth, capital development, and performance in international sports and academic competitions, Teacher Yu chooses to interpret the "Chinese Aura" as a beacon of inspiration encouraging Chinese educators to offer culturally relevant education.

For Teacher Yu, "Chinese Aura" is an umbrella term for manifestations of desirable Chinese traits. It is more an expression than a concept. It depicts phenomena and courses of action with discernible Chinese characteristics, something that is imbedded in the culture and history of the country. He recalls his discovery of the meaning of "Chinese Aura" during a 10-day trip in 2006 to Yan'an, the "Mecca of the Chinese Revolution," where he was inspired by a recorded remark by Chairman Mao: "We need to use theories and ideas with Chinese character, Chinese style, and Chinese form to guide the revolution in China" (Interview 2, 2014: 5). He spent the rest of the Yan'an trip searching for an understanding of "unique Chinese characteristics." He confides: "I pondered the meaning of 'Chinese Aura'. What did it mean when we said something had Chinese characteristics? And what about this reference to Chinese form?" (Ibid.). He claims that he finally realized that "unique Chinese characteristics" were to be found in the lives of the common people in many localities. He recalls:

> When you see the waist drums that people carry, the white scarves that they wear about their heads, and hear the Shaanbei (Northern Shaanxi) folk songs that they sing, you know it's the [cultural] form of Northern Shaanxi Province. And when you see their art of paper cutting, you know it's not American, and it's not Italian. It's undoubtedly Chinese. Through this kind of observation, I developed a deeper understanding of Chinese character, Chinese style, and Chinese form. (Ibid.)

The realization that all human activities can be traced back to their indigenous roots has allowed Teacher Yu to appreciate the essentiality of culture in educational undertakings. He believes that "for anything to survive and grow, it has to be connected to its own roots, to the indigenous. This includes education" (Ibid.: 6). The kind of culturally anchored education that Teacher Yu envisages is one that will be grounded in the traditions of China. "Its problems will arise from Chinese [reality], its theoretical resources will be Chinese, based on Chinese logic, and articulated in the Chinese language" (Interview 4, 2014: 1). He uses an excerpt from *Xueji*, an ancient Chinese commentary on teaching and learning, to illustrate the enduring influence of culture on education: "'Teaching and learning promote and enhance each other' ('zhangshan jiushi') and 'focus on the strengths students use in order to overcome their shortcomings' ('jiaoxue xiangzhang') are old maxims that are currently popular, but they can be traced back to [the ancient text of] *Xueji*"[5] (Ibid.).

The same concern for education's indigenous roots is also evident in Teacher Yu's views on the direction of educational research. He says: "Educational research has to be rooted in China. The research problems should be Chinese. Its mode of expression should be Chinese. Its theoretical resources should be related to China, or be modified in accordance with the situation in China" (Interview 2, 2014: 17). He is concerned over the idle and lofty speculations that dot the landscapes of contemporary educational research. Regarding the societal relevance of educational inquiry, he argues that "if the research problems are divorced from the reality of China, it would be impossible to address the salient problems that Chinese education is facing today" (Ibid.: 16). As far as the methods of inquiry are concerned, Teacher Yu holds an inclusive view and seems to trust the effectiveness of certain Western methods. His growing interest in conducting locally relevant research has drawn his attention to the integration of life history and intellectual history for the exploration of educational thinkers. For example, he is currently conducting a study on the life history of his mentor, Prof. Wang, which requires him to venture into field research that will be conducted at different localities. He highlights his plans enthusiastically:

> The film crew [of the research project] will depart soon. We'll visit and interview at least ten people [in various places], including his hometown. We want to find out why my teacher had developed such ideas, and how these ideas are related to his intellectual history. And in what ways do others view his ideas. I think we lack this kind of research in China. I feel that this research project [of mine] is deeply influenced by Pinar. Pinar advocates this kind of autobiographical research. It's not just autobiographical, not just about him, but we also need to conduct research on him. What was his calling? It was the way that life history and intellectual history interact. (Ibid.:17).

In his treatment of indigenous and Western knowledge, Teacher Yu distinguishes those ideas and practices that are grounded in the societal context of China from those that are imported from the West. In a way, his treatment of the two kinds of knowledge harks back to an old principle, which was laid down by Chinese reformers a 100 years ago, that indigenous Chinese knowledge should provide the core substance of thinking while Western knowledge should be used as methods and tools. When placed on a continuum of societal development, the two kinds of knowledge will each have a different role to play: Indigenous knowledge, which is nurtured by Chinese culture through time, will serve as the principal source, and Western knowledge, which is adopted to serve the needs of the country's modernization projects, will serve as the secondary source. As an education theorist, Teacher Yu is convinced that all educational ideas "are nurtured in the 'womb of culture' … the cultural dimensions that are embedded in educational theories provide them with deeper meanings. [This cultural substance] is the 'soul' of a culture that profoundly influences the [construction] of the nation and the shaping of national character" (Yu and Li 2010: 17).

The development of educational studies as an academic discipline, however, has strayed from the path that Chinese reformers had envisaged. Teacher Yu thinks that the problems rest in the process by which foreign knowledge is imported and the disparities between the maturation of the knowledge systems in China and the West. "[Western educational studies] has gone through the developmental stages of pre-discipline, independence of discipline, and disciplinary network," he explains, "and this has allowed educational studies [in the West] to mature with [the support] of comprehensive educational knowledge" (Ibid.: 21). For Teacher Yu, the development of educational studies in China has never had a chance to mature because "it was driven by a pragmatic rationality of national survival and saving the country, and the importation and transplantation of foreign theories has never ceased" (Ibid.). With the importation of Western educational knowledge from a "matured" knowledge base, the "still maturing" Chinese educational discourse is overcome by the powerful structure that supports the narrative of Western educational studies, including research paradigms, methods, and publications. Teacher Yu elaborates:

Within the [Western] structure are sub-fields of inquiry and modes of research that the less mature research collective [in China] is trying to imitate. Through journals and books, [Western epistemological substance] is disseminated and permeates the younger [Chinese] academic community, and thereby absorbing the educational research of this still maturing collective into the structure of mainstream discourse. From there, the autonomous research consciousness [of the growing collective] as well as its ability to foster its own discourse will be lost. (Ibid.)

Teacher Yu is wary of the uncritical adoption of Western educational ideas and practices in the Chinese scholarly community, especially when admiration of foreign practices may stem from the dissatisfaction with certain shortcomings of indigenous education or problems in societal projects (Yu and Qin 2009: 28). He allows that "where theory and practice are underdeveloped, it is not unusual to have superficial efforts in the indigenization of educational theories and a lack of attention given to unearthing [research] problems from indigenous practices. The scarcity of indigenous [research] problems in turn hampers efforts in the indigenization of educational theories" (Ibid.).

Teacher Yu's insistence on preserving Chinese character in the development of educational studies in China is not based on a simple patriotic consideration. He actually thinks that it is the only way that the field can hope to achieve some kind of independence in the world of scholarship. The emphasis on projecting a "Chinese Aura" for national development is to ensure that related endeavors will have a "soul" that embodies indigenous cultural meanings.

HARMONIOUS CONVERGENCE UNDER THE MEAN

Given the tensions that exist in the interaction between tradition and modernity and between the indigenous and the foreign, how should Chinese educators make sense of the interplay of these forces in their work?

To allow Chinese educators to work amid the tensions created by forces of change, Teacher Yu suggests a Chinese approach to solving educational problems in a Chinese context. He advocates fostering harmony amid the tensions. His suggestion is to alleviate the burden of discord between the forces that are at work in the process of educational change in China. As a scholar who believes that "the choices that we made are inevitably linked to the history of our times" (Interview 4, 2014: 9), and that "good scholarly inquiry should have a sense of history" (Interview 3, 2014: 4), he is keenly aware of the historical circumstances under which the interplay between the change forces took place. His proposed solution, fostering harmony amid tensions, is grounded in an understanding of the modern and contemporary history of Chinese education.

In China, the modern schools and universities that were established at the beginning of the twentieth century were products of a "national salvation" process that aimed to save the country from foreign aggression and national disintegration. The government of China dispatched youths to study abroad, borrowed from the educational experiences of industrialized countries (Hayhoe and Bastid 1987), and tried to nurture the kinds of talent that would transform its modernization blueprint into reality. Today, education is still being seen as a vehicle for national development, and the urgency for quick results lingers in the education sector. It is from this historical perspective that Teacher Yu proposes using the concept of "Harmony and Integration" ("hehe"), which was originally used to depict harmony in nature, as a guide for dealing with the transformation of Chinese education. For the application of this concept, he refers once again to the tenets of the *Book of the Mean*, which counsels moderation and appropriateness.

The concept of "Harmony and Integration" is envisioned by Teacher Yu to fulfill concord and agreement between change forces that are at work in the education sector. These forces influence the outlook of its stakeholders and affect their educational choices. In the cultural context of China, "Harmony" denotes concord, peace, and auspicious tranquility, while "Integration" means unity, assimilation, and cooperation. Teacher Yu first applies this concept to the contesting ideas of modernity and postmodernity. He argues that they are actually a pair, twin concepts, in the societal development of China: Modernity provides the goals, direction, and principles for the modernization project which is still incomplete, and postmodernity delineates the problems of modernity and the social consequences that negligence would bring. For him, theories of postmodernism illuminate "the differences and diversity in our culture." He says:

> [In China] the Northeast culture is different from the Northwest culture; and it's different from the Southeast culture as well. It's like people's taste. There are regional differences in people's preferences. We can't say that differences are wrong and sameness is good. I think that one of the positive contributions of postmodernism to our society and education is that it makes us respect differences and tolerate diversity. There are commonalities among certain good things in the world, but they can't be exactly the same. (Interview 5, 2016: 6–7)

However, Teacher Yu is keenly aware of the disparities that exist in the society. In Chinese education, postmodernity heralds the challenges that await solutions. For this reason, he points to the needs for more tolerance of diversity and for respect of "others" (Interview 3, 2014: 10). He believes that education has an important role to play in improving social conditions.

The "harmonious convergence" of modernity and postmodernity that Teacher Yu envisages will only be possible if the people in charge of education are willing to modify their outlook so as to allow certain features of the postmodernist critique to be integrated into its further development. An "organic integration" of postmodernist ideas (Yu 2005: 55) will require more inclusive policies to be put in place so that the present modernist approach can be modified to accommodate the needs of diversity, such as special needs education and increased opportunities for the disadvantaged. Such a change in thinking will better prepare Chinese education to evaluate, critique, and rejuvenate itself (Ibid.).

The same can be said about the "harmonious convergence" of domestic change forces, such as the integration of tradition and modernity in education. Unlike the integration of postmodernist ideas, which is about adding something new to the education agenda, the interplay between tradition and modernity is about preserving thinking and practices in the educational context. Through time, Chinese education has retained many traditional characteristics as it modernized, such as deference toward teachers and reliance on public examinations as a selection tool. By tapping into ancient wisdom to address contemporary issues, Teacher Yu elucidates its relevance and admonishes educators and policymaker on the danger of mindlessly replacing old, traditional practices with new, modern measures.

The "harmonious convergence" of indigenous and foreign change forces in education presents a different set of problems for which policy alone may not be a sufficient solution. Convergence of change forces, in this case, will be dependent on the openness of the local system and the attitudinal readiness of local stakeholders. Fundamentally, it is their treatment of the novel ideas and practices of the "other" that determines the outcomes of convergence. In a closed system where stakeholders are resistant to change, convergence will be difficult to accomplish. Conversely, where stakeholders are willing to take a broad view of their place in the world, the system will be able to transcend the simple process of incorporating foreign matters and be able to address global educational issues, such as environmental education and world citizenship.

Teacher Yu thinks that the immediate task is to make people aware of the "other" and to learn how to cooperate with other people. He argues that the perception of "'I' in relation to 'others' is a big problem because it involves ethical and political issues." For the Chinese, "others" are always a mystery. "So getting inside [the mind] of another person, and understanding them is a problem." He elaborates:

> We Chinese say that it is easy to know people's faces but not their hearts. This tells us how difficult it is to really understand a person. But it is so hard to divorce yourself from others now, especially with current communications. In the past, people could live by themselves. But you can't do anything if you withdraw from others now. We have reached an age when we can't help but be dependent on others; yet we want to isolate ourselves at the same time. We'd rather endure loneliness. It's an intriguing age. Isn't it? [I mean dealing with] 'others'.... It is a salient problem now, especially in this age of globalization, in the Internet age. (Interview 3, 2014: 10)

The change forces generated by globalization and digitization have made relational conditions of human interaction much more complicated. In education, knowing and understanding "others" are a prerequisite for the acceptance of novel ideas and practices from people who are different. The tasks of integrating new ways of thinking and doing into the existing system are important steps toward his vision of "harmonious convergence." He asks: "How do we cooperate with others? How do we co-exist with others, including people from other countries, those of a different race, and those with different religious beliefs? In sum, how do we deal with ... the 'other'?" (Interview 2, 2014: 13).

A more ambitious goal for Chinese education, according to Teacher Yu's vision, is the creation of a global outlook for the citizenry of China that people would consider themselves as citizens of the world who are willing to shoulder certain global responsibilities. Such responsibilities will include "environmental protection and combat of terrorism, for the age of the global village has arrived" (Interview 2, 2014: 16). For the Chinese to fulfill these responsibilities, it is essential that they learn to respect the environment and needs of people in other countries. He cautions:

The corporations of China shouldn't damage the environment abroad. I think about this problem because we now have corporations [conducting business] overseas. Some of them went to Africa and Myanmar, saw their good wood, cut down the trees, dragged the wood back here and sold it for money. I think if we look at this [kind of action] from the perspective of a Chinese citizen, we may think that it's no big problem. But if look at it from the perspective of a world citizen, I guarantee that it's definitely a problem. We're forbidden to hunt tigers here in China. So we shouldn't go overseas and shoot others' tigers. That's why I think we need to give up the narrow China [perspective] and move toward the world. (Ibid.)

Tolerance of differences and acceptance of novelty are the essential ingredients for "harmonious convergence" to take effect in the education sector. For Teacher Yu, the possibility of convergence will be determined by the degree of local acceptance of Western ideas and practices. Much will depend on the willingness and capacity of the Chinese education sector to absorb them. He thinks that authentic convergence will take place when Western knowledge is modified and accepted as an integral part of local education. There is an "in-between space" between the realms of theory and practice where Western educational theories can be organically converted to suit the indigenous context. The successful conversion for indigenization may result in a transformation of originally Western ideas into "regenerated" Chinese ones (Yu and Li 2010: 22). In this sense, the convergence of the foreign and the indigenous requires a process of modification where transplanted Western ideas are validated by local practices. The validity of Western knowledge has to be verified through the continuous scrutiny of research, including action research that can observe its effectiveness in action (Ibid.: 23). Thus, the integration of Western ideas and practices into local educational settings is more than simply inserting them into the Chinese educational vocabulary. It requires an appropriate adoption of Western knowledge in the Chinese context. So what does "appropriate" mean? Are there principles of "appropriateness" to which we can refer? Teacher Yu proposes that we can find them in the *Book of the Mean*, as readers will now be aware that it is one of his favorite sources of Confucian wisdom.

According to the *Book of the Mean*, human beings should strive to maintain a state of constant equilibrium in their minds so that they can live a balanced life and sustain a harmonious relationship with nature and other people. "The mean" is the appropriate middle ground between extremities, a desirable state that affords a balanced approach to life (Zhang et al. 2001: 39–40). On a personal level, "the mean" should guide a person's speech and action, ensuring that due attention be given to the constraints embedded in a situation, including the mores of human relations. The guidance of "the mean" warrants appropriate behavior. Moreover, "the mean" is also being considered as a personal virtue.[6] The appropriate treatment of others requires empathy, while decisions to be made should be based on a cognitive and affective understanding of persons that will be affected by them. On a systemic level, "the mean" should be applied to the formulation of educational policies. "Don't take extreme measures" and "allow for the emergence of unforeseen problems" are Teacher Yu's advices to those seeking to change the education system (Interview 4, 2014: 3). To achieve balance and harmony within the system, he counsels against the imposition of draconian measures that will disrupt its equilibrium. On this kind of situation, he makes idiomatic references to those well-intended policies that push educational reform to an idealized extreme: "Water in its purest cannot sustain fish," and "A person who scrutinizes too carefully will be without friends." For this reason, he urges restraint and moderation in the implementation of reform and objects to "radical changes" (Ibid.: 4). For educational undertakings, then, the application of the principle of appropriateness requires a careful examination of the constraints embedded in the context of education with serious consideration being given to factors that affect people's well-being. The kind of measures that emerge from such an application should allow educators and policymakers to look beyond the superficial account of student achievement figures and arrive at a better understanding of their work.

Teacher Yu's extends his advocacy of the tenets of the *Book of the Mean* beyond the confines of education to include all forms of human action. He appreciates the possibility of "the mean" serving as a beacon of civility and considers that the maintenance of harmony and balance in people's lives should be the developmental goal of society and education. This perhaps explains his emphasis on "the need for the Chinese people to learn to comply with civic norms and rules," which convey the appropriate standard of social behavior (Interview 2, 2014: 18) and his hope that Chinese education will nurture "people who can cultivate peace and harmony in their lives" (Interview 5, 2016: 6). For Teacher Yu, "the mean" provides the basis for measuring the appropriateness of human action (Interview 4, 2014: 3), and it is by the requisite principles of appropriateness that the outcomes of human action, both personal and collective, should be judged.

By illuminating the tenets of the *Book of the Mean*, Teacher Yu paves the way for the convergence of change forces on a visionary platform of "Harmony and Integration." The modernization of Chinese society and education will be made possible by "harmonious convergence," with "the mean" providing the framework of appropriate actions. Teacher Yu prefers to see societal development as the embodiment of gradual and methodical processes that are bolstered by tolerance and leniency (*kuan-rong*), a quality of openness and forbearance that will make "harmonious convergence" plausible. Indeed, he has learned the importance of tolerance and leniency through lived experiences in schooling, work, and life. He has seen how new ideas, imported or homegrown, have transformed people's worldview (Interview 4, 2014: 8). As an educator, he must have realized that tolerance of differences and diversity could be taught, and leniency is human compassion that could be nurtured. However, one wonders whether a revival of the ethos of tolerance and leniency can provide the necessary conditions for the "harmonious convergence" of change forces, notwithstanding the impressive accomplishments in Chinese society and education.

As an observer of history who professes faith in the efficacy of policies and institutions in solving societal problems, Teacher Yu is probably assuming that the exercise to integrate change forces will be supported by appropriate official measures. Nevertheless, the complexity created by such change forces, most of which have emerged since the implementation of the "open-door" policy of the 1980s, has caused the transformation of society and education. For example, the popularization of Western literature and arts has ushered in the concept of "I" and facilitated the discovery of the centrality of the individual. Moreover, the importation of Western educational ideas presented an alternative model of educating to a school system that operates on the principles of uniformity. These ideas also expedited curriculum reform in China. Furthermore, the growing importance of Western knowledge and practices presents a challenge to the conventional wisdom that they should remain mere instruments for China's modernization projects. The change forces that drive society and education are not limited to those influences that were imported from abroad. As Chinese society changes with impressive economic growth, and the expectations of its people surpass what modernization can offer, the management of China's vast population becomes a herculean task. Postmodernist demands for social justice, individual freedom, and fair treatment for marginalized groups simmer beneath a thin layer of shibboleths lauding social harmony, economic prosperity, and national competitiveness. In education, the plight of the impoverished and undereducated is obscured by the academic prowess that is demonstrated by selected students in international testing contests.

The national project of continual development, therefore, requires a kind of vision that can embody social and political progress at home and global stability abroad. One wonders what kind of strategies that "Harmony and Integration" may yield, and whether "Chinese Aura" would have an audience in the arena of international politics.

NOTES

1. The quotation is cited in *Zheng Yu* (translated as *Discourses of the State of Zheng*), which is a section in *Guo Yu* (translated as *Discourses of the States*). *Guo Yu* is a collection of narratives and dialogues involving the rulers, their advisors, and various historical figures in eight states in the Spring and Autumn period (770–476 BCE). The authorship of the ancient text is sometimes attributed Zuo Qiuming (*circa* 502–422 BCE), a well-known historian. It is widely believed that *Guo Yu* is the earliest comprehensive collection of histories of individual states in China. Partial English translation of *Guo Yu* can be found in Wang, H. (2012).
2. "Using the deeds of others as a mirror, we can understand our own achievements and fallacies." This maxim was widely attributed to Li Shimin (posthumous title Tang Taizong, 598–649 AD) who was recognized as one of the most powerful emperors in Chinese history.
3. The term was coined by Zhang Zhidong (1837–1909), a key reformer who served in the rapidly declining imperial court of the Qing Dynasty in the nineteenth century. Weakened by the encroachment of Western powers, the government tried to find ways to tap foreign technological wisdom without undermining the centrality of Chinese culture and values in national development. Zhang's thesis of demarcating the purpose and utility of knowledge in national development was widely circulated among reformers. It is still deemed relevant to the situation in China today. For an examination of Zhang's influence on Chinese education, see Ayers (1971).
4. "China Aura" emerged as an umbrella term for the country's many accomplishments in recent years. In a sense, it is an end product of the "open-door" policies of the 1980s when China re-emerged in international affairs as a poor and backward country. Rapid economic growth and significant

achievements in major areas of development, such as the success of its space program and in international competitions of various kinds, have bred self-confidence and national pride among the populace. "China Aura" is a grandiloquent way of describing things with Chinese characteristics.

5. *Xueji*, translated by James Legge as "Record on the Subject of Education," is an essay on teaching and learning which represents a statement of Confucian philosophy of education. It was canonized as a fascicle in *Liji* ("The Book of Rites"), which outlined various aspects of the basic curriculum of Confucian education. *Xueji* is one of the earliest essays to discuss the philosophy, principles, and methods of teaching and learning as well as the roles of teachers and students in ancient China. For an examination of the contemporary relevance of *Xueji* from the perspectives of philosophy and education, see Xu and McEwan (2016).

6. The postulation of "the mean" as a personal virtue, as articulated in the *Book of the Mean*, affords a philosophical parallel to Aristotle's doctrine on the same subject. For Aristotle, virtues lie between the states of excess and deficiency. He posited that the mean was to be determined after a thoughtful process that took into account the particular circumstances affecting the individual. This postulation is similar to that which is proposed in the Confucian *Book of the Mean*. See, for example, Kraut (2014), Yu (2007).

References

Ayers, W. (1971). *Chang Chih-tung and educational reform in China.* Cambridge, MA: Harvard University Press.

Hayhoe, R., & Bastid, M. (Eds.). (1987). *China's education and the industrialized world: Studies in cultural transfer.* Armonk, NY: M.E. Sharpe.

Kraut, R. (2014). Aristotle's Ethics, *The Stanford Encyclopedia of Philosophy* (Summer 2014 Edition). Retrieved April 21, 2015, from http://plato.stanford.edu/archives/sum2014/entries/aristotle-ethics/.

Pinar, W. F. (1975). *The method of "Currere".* Paper presented at the annual meeting of the American Educational Research Association in 1975, Washington, DC. Cited in ERIC: ED104766.

Wang, H. (Trans.) (2012). *The discourses of the states.* Changsha: Hunan People's Publishing House.

Xu, D., & McEwan, H. (Eds.). (2016). *Chinese philosophy on teaching and learning: Xueji in the twenty-first century.* Albany, NY: State University of New York Press.

Yu, W. (2005). Jiaoyuguan de xiandaixing weiji yu xinlujing chutan [Modernity crisis of educational perspectives and research on the new route]. *Jiaoyu Yanjiu [Educational Research]*, *3*, 51–57.

Yu, J. Y. (2007). *The ethics of Confucius and Aristotle: Mirrors of virtue.* New York: Routledge.

Yu, W., & Y. Y. Qin. (2009). Bentu wenti yishi yu jiaoyu lilun bentuhua [Local issue awareness and the localization of educational theory]. *Jiaoyu Yanjiu [Educational Research]*, *6*, 27–31.

Yu, W., & S. S. Li. (2010). Jiaoyu lilun bentuhua de sange qiantixing wenti [On the three preliminary issues of localization of educational theory]. *Jiaoyu Yanjiu [Educational Research]*, *4*, 17–24.

Zhang, D. S., Y. J. Jin, H. W. Chen, J. M. Chen, Z. F. Yang, Z. Y. Zhao, & S. B. Yi. (2001). Lun Zhong Yong lixing: Gongju lixing, jiazhi lixing, he goutong lixing zhiwei [On *Zhongyong* rationality: Beyond instrumental rationality, value rationality, and communicative rationality]. *Shehuixue Yanjiu [Studies in Sociology]*, *2*, 33–48.

CHAPTER 5

Navigating Educational Change

Abstract The professor has made career changes that required altera-tions of his role and identity at the university and in the scholarly world. Issues surrounding these changes are discussed in relation to China's educational transformation. The circumstances underlying his choice of career paths and professional pursuits delineate the kind of opportunities and challenges that are embedded in Chinese organization and society. The narrative of his experiences at different academic and administrative positions sheds light on the confidence behind his readiness to take on novel duties and the assertion of agency while he was serving a range of interests. It also provides a snapshot of the ladder of success in Chinese higher education and offers lessons in docility and compliance.

Keywords Educational change in China · University administration Career advancement · Leadership in Chinese university

During his career, Teacher Yu has made significant changes in his role and identity at the university and in the scholarly world. How do changes in his career relate to China's educational transformation and its ascension on the international stage? What motivated him to choose the career paths that have shaped his identity?

Teacher Yu's story about changes in his family, university, and com-munity reflects the kind of opportunities and challenges that are found in the fluid context of contemporary Chinese society. For the ordinary

F. Wang and L.N.K. Lo, *Navigating Educational Change in China*, Curriculum Studies Worldwide, DOI 10.1007/978-3-319-63615-3_5

93

Chinese citizens who have grown up in China under the "open-door" policies of the 1980s, power, wealth, and social advancement await those who can successfully complete their journey through the formal educational system. Before that, in the dark days of political campaigns against the intellectuals, scholarly and artistic pursuits might lead to misfortunes. The fate of the educated seemed to have been left to the broad sweep of history that oscillates uneasily, and sometimes violently, between contesting human beliefs and actions. The transformation of contemporary China, therefore, provides a context for Teacher Yu's experiences in life and work.

A Portrait of Career Transitions in Changing Educational Contexts

In the first 30 years of the People's Republic, education under Communism was in a constant state of flux. The ambition of the ruling regime to develop education along the principles of nationalism, scientism, and populism in the largest education experiment in human history ended in continuous instability and chaos (Hu 1974). The dysfunctional education system was governed by inertia and fear.

During periods of radical politics, educational policies bred unorthodox forms of organization, administration, and pedagogy that were daring attempts in mixing indigenous knowledge with the energy of the common people. For example, the "red and expert universities" that were popular during the Great Leap Forward (1958–1959) epitomized a populist scheme to provide education at the worksite for workers who had received little schooling. The administration of schools and universities by "revolutionary committees" consisting of workers, peasants, and soldiers during the Cultural Revolution was an assurance against the perpetration of bourgeois thinking of intellectuals and teachers (Chen 1974). The many work-and-study programs during the Cultural Revolution, popularized by such project as the Chaoyang Agricultural College, represented a vision that teaching and learning had to be based on the reality of work (Ibid.). The aforementioned experiments had exploited the vigor of non-education forces in the workplace and community for education projects in creative ways, but, taken as a whole, their fleeting brilliance could only be considered sparks in the dark days of education in China.

Teacher Yu did not have to suffer the deprivation of formal schooling because he was too young to have experienced the mass panic of the Great Leap Forward when millions starved. Before he could remember the ugly confrontations of Red Guards as a boy, the childhood memories that he related were days of making toy tanks and carefree plays under the care of his grandmother. The fondest of his childhood moments was when his father, a factory worker, took him to a parade of the local militia. Sitting on his father's shoulders, he watched admiringly the people carrying guns that displayed their power and readiness to defend his community. The chaos that ensued during the early part of the Cultural Revolution left a strong imprint on his mind that led him to speculate, decades later, on the "banality of evil" in Chinese society. Yet, he and his family were fortunate to be spared from the personal suffering and humiliation that so many had suffered. By the time he reached school-attending age in the 1970s, some of the schools were reopened, thus affording a chance for him to receive some kind of formal education as we understand schooling to be today.

Today, many Chinese higher institutions are led and managed by persons who are around the same age as Teacher Yu, who was born in the 1960s. As a distinct generation of Chinese academics, they have witnessed widespread political turbulence and also unprecedented economic growth. They are the beneficiaries of a revived university system that admitted students through a competitive system-wide examination. They were educated by a generation of scholar-teachers who witnessed the changeover of political regimes, and some of them had personally suffered purges during politically radical times, being forced into a kind of "academic exile" that accounted for a costly hiatus in the lineage of Chinese scholarship. One of Teacher Yu's academic mentors, Prof. Wang, was an exemplar of intellectual integrity. Like many scholars of his generation, he suffered humiliation during the Cultural Revolution, and he was criticized again even in the 1980s, a period that Teacher Yu deemed to be a decade of liberalization in Chinese society and education. From the experience of an unyielding scholar-teacher like Prof. Wang, perhaps a lesson of survival in the Chinese academia could be learned that intellectual prowess, as demonstrated by the elegance of reasons, could never prevail over administrative mandates, as sanctioned within the reach of state power. When the consequences of this one-sided match of strengths become clear to all players, their future efforts to gain recognition would be invested in refining the art of docility.

China's approach toward liberalization in the 1980s was accentuated by the "open-door" policy of the party-state that signified China's entry into the world community. It was a serious attempt to free the country from the quagmire of self-imposed isolation and underdevelopment. Systemic reforms for modernization were formulated and implemented. In higher education, the foundation of further development was laid when the first class of university students was admitted into the universities that reopened toward the end of the 1970s. The spirit of renewal was rekindled by the emergence of fresh scholarly debates, new art forms, and literary works that reflected the excitement of discovery. For Teacher Yu, the 1980s marked the advent of a cultural renaissance that was rarely seen in contemporary Chinese history.

Be that as it may, the contest between foreign and indigenous thinking continued to create tensions in the society and polity. Choices between traditional and modern methods of maintaining stability and creating wealth for the nation produced discord among officials and intellectuals. As China moved through different phases of modernization, the social and economic conditions of the country demanded a new kind of human resources that could take the country to a higher level of societal development. The education system expanded rapidly as demands for a better-trained workforce continued to grow. The party-state formally initiated a system-wide educational reform in 1985 (CCCPC 1985). Efforts to address such important issues as the expansion of opportunities in basic education, the autonomy of higher institutions, and the responsibility and accountability of school leaders were integral parts of a blueprint for a modern system of education. The endeavor to enact laws for compulsory schooling, higher education, and teachers was also a part of that modernization plan. By the time when the concept of "quality education" was introduced as an antithesis of "exam-oriented education" in the late 1990s, Chinese education was ready for a transformation since the necessary groundwork was laid.

The process of transformation of Chinese education began with the cautious acceptance of Western ideas and practices and a willingness to participate in educational affairs of the world. This departure from its past isolationist stance was apparent in the systemic curriculum reform that was initiated at the advent of the new century. The curriculum reform was based on the assumption that education was to serve the all-round development of the child with pedagogical approaches that appeared novel to educators at the time. Student learning was to become the center of the pedagogy, and learning was to be achieved through guided exploration rather than by the direct instruction of teachers. There was to be less emphasis on examinations, less homework, and more time and space for individual exploration. In an educational system where the presence of the state was ubiquitous, where administration management was patriarchal, and where the influence of examinations was deeply rooted, the progressive overtones of curriculum reform seemed almost ironic.

The spirit of experimentation in education and the excitement that surrounded the implementation of educational reform did have a clear influence on Teacher Yu's decision to work at the university after graduation. At the time, with the gradual demise of the unified job assignment system, which mandatorily dispatched university graduates to work in state-controlled organizations such as higher institutions, state enterprises, and governmental bureaus, the career choices of a university graduate like Teacher Yu became more open. Among the career paths afforded by the government, businesses, and higher institutions, he chose to stay and work for his *alma mater*. Teacher Yu's early career choice of staying in academia seems to suit the disposition of a person who liked to read, could spend a lot of time in solitude, and was familiar with the university setting. He served as a student counselor, a job that classified him as a "political worker." His position was neither administrative nor academic. In a status conscious workplace like the university, this kind of obscure appointment would not have sat well with those looking for opportunities to get ahead. At a time when some of his fellow graduates were seeking other avenues of employment, Teacher Yu's decision to work as a student counselor in a familiar environment might have been seen as a sign of complacency or an indication of strong affinity toward the university, or both. However, beyond the plain display of institutional loyalty lies a deeper appreciation of his employment. Being a student counselor, Teacher Yu found meaning in his work. He once described his job as being a "king of children." In fact, being with people who were slightly younger in age, he developed as a person on the job as he grew with his students, learned to investigate the newest ideas that inspired them, and tried to help alleviate their growing pains (Interview 2, 2014: 23–27).

There were certain aspects of the job that must have unsettled Teacher Yu, for they forced him to confront the reality of Chinese education whenever draconian measures were being imposed on the student body during politically radical times. He cited as an example the mandatory military training that all new university students had to endure (Interview 2, 2014: 15). For as much as Teacher Yu has wanted to remember the 1980s as a time of openness and freedom, Chinese universities and schools have had to operate under the shadow of continuous political campaigns during that decade, such as the Anti-Spiritual Pollution Campaign in 1983 and the Anti-Bourgeois Liberalization Campaign in 1987. These political quandaries, as well as the crisis that surrounded the suppression of student activism in the late 1980s, would have forced any student counselor into the horn of an identity dilemma with the questions: "Who am I?" and "What is the purpose of my work?" Teacher Yu continued to serve as a "political worker" for several more years. Perhaps he was able to transcend the currents of politics with the strengths that he deduced from the meaning of his work, by doing something good for his students.

At the advent of the new century, the party-state renewed its drive to implement a system-wide curriculum reform in the schools. The ensuing debates on the meaning and effectiveness of the new curriculum reform exemplified the disagreement between the traditional and reformist views on what should be learned in schools. Arguments presented in the most heated debate centered on the purpose of the curriculum which, as the defenders of traditional educational values had insisted, should be designed for the construction of a strong knowledge base through the acquisition of subject knowledge. This was contrary to the reformist views which attempted to guide the curriculum toward the integration of subject knowledge with an approach that encouraged cross-disciplinary understanding and active investigation into matters that are relevant to the lives of the students.

The progressive ideas behind curriculum reform trace their theoretical origins to Western educational thinkers such as Pestalozzi, Parker, Dewey, and more. The adoption of Western ideas and practices in education came as a result of two decades of engagement with Western institutions and scholarship. The "open-door" policy allowed a significant increase in academic exchange activities, overseas faculty visits, and student pursuance of further study in Western countries. Those who came home with newly found knowledge contributed to a new perspective on educational aims and practices. The influence of Western thinking on the reformers undoubtedly left its imprints on their proposals for change. China's participation in international affairs yielded comparisons with advanced industrial societies that delineated the impediments to its educational progress; yet, they have also shown the areas in which China has been among the world's leaders. The impressive growth of the economy, the admission into the World Trade Organization in 2001, the hosting of the Olympic Games in 2008, and the success of its space exploration program have elevated China's national pride to a new height. Amid the optimism, a term "Chinese Aura" (*Zhongguo qipai*) was invented to magnify the country's exceptionality and newly found status in the world. The aspiration to greatness even led the leadership of the party-state to conceive yet another slogan, "Chinese Dream" (*Zhongguo meng*).

Translated into educational reality, the "Chinese Aura" phenomenon was clearly discernible in the creation of "world-class" universities. In line with past strategies that allowed "certain people to get rich first," a few higher institutions with exceptional strengths were selected for focused investment in order to propel them to the highest echelon of research universities in the world. The "world-class universities" project began in 1998, and eventually, 39 of China's 2542 higher education institutions were given extra funding earmarked for diverse purposes, including international exchange, collaborative research, and recruitment of foreign students and faculty. After close to two decades of experimentation, it is still unclear whether China's top institutions have been able to grow a national character that could make them representatives of "Chinese Aura." By pumping more resources into its top universities, China has managed to feed a couple of institutions into the world's top universities, according to various university ranking agencies. But the lop-sided allocation of resources in favor of the richest few has caused its higher education sector to become more stratified and inequitable. As a way to strengthen their international standing, the top universities are encouraging their faculty to engage in joint ventures with foreign institutions and to publish the fruit of their inquiry in indexed foreign journals that are based mostly in the West. Murmurs of dissent can now be heard among young faculty whose tenure and upward mobility have become dependent on their ability to tailor their wisdom to the conventional format of Western scholarship[1] and on their publication record in foreign journals. In a sense, the "world-class universities" project, which was designed to project the country's "Chinese Aura" to the world, has not been able to illuminate the national character of China's top universities; rather, the project has caused the unintended consequences of internal disparity and the undesirable submission to the power and norms of Western scholarship.

Changes in higher education affected the developmental direction of all institutions, which were compelled to respond to the demands of change in order to maintain their own competitive edge in funding procurement and institutional ranking. An atmosphere of relentless competition permeated the system of higher education, and Teacher Yu's university, which was an institution known for its achievements in teacher education and educational studies, could ill-afford to stay aloof from the race for status and survival. Aside from performing the usual duties as an institution of higher learning such as the dissemination and advancement of knowledge, the university was charged with the added responsibilities of participating in research and development projects that affected the nation's schools. Like other institutions that had to operate under strong financial pressures, the university decided to move toward the education market when large-scale retraining of teachers became a mandatory national policy. As institutional ranking became a highly contested exercise in which major fields of study were being assessed individually, the university had to protect the advantageous positions of its key subjects by boosting productivity in those areas of strength. All of these changes provided opportunities for Teacher Yu to make certain career changes that facilitated his advancement.

With the professional capital and connections that he had accumulated during a decade of service as a "political worker," Teacher Yu could have strived to become a high-level Party functionary at the university. In Chinese institutions, Party functionaries often enjoy equal, if not higher, status than their colleagues in the academic stream. Yet, personnel reshuffles at the university have assigned him to different positions that offered new opportunities for advancement.

Teacher Yu's appointment to the directorship of the Rural Education Research Institute in 2005 came at a time when the party-state was growing increasingly concerned over the underdevelopment of rural education. It was also apparent that the progress of its system-wide curriculum reform had come to a standstill. The Institute's director left the university for another institution after a tenure of 7 years. Teacher Yu's subsequent appointment as the director of the School of Distance Education was made in 2007, in the heyday of marketization in higher education, when self-financing programs of all kinds sprang up in response expanding social demands for further education. The university needed an enterprising officer to head up such a unit, and he was assigned to the position. For Teacher Yu, becoming increasingly aware of the power of the Internet, the headship of a unit that focused its business on distance education challenged him to experiment and innovate.

Later in his career, the appointment to the deanship of the Faculty of Education in 2012 came after the unit underwent a major reorganization, an exercise that was purportedly designed to enhance its effectiveness. The reorganization was initiated amid official calls for better governance and in the face of mounting pressure from competing institutions vying for more recognition and funding. The outgoing dean had just completed his two terms, having served for 10 years. By being assigned to the headship of one of the most important units of the university, Teacher Yu was supposed to lead the Faculty of Education into a new era.

His newest appointment as the principal of the university's affiliated primary school was made in 2014 when the role of elite schools in China was viewed somewhat critically through an increasingly egalitarian lens. With the party-state calling for more equity in education, and with the implementation of certain state policies that would no longer favor the elite schools, the primary school was in need of a leader with the necessary knowledge and skills to fend off anti-elitist criticism, on the one hand, and to secure the support of the parents and community, on the other hand. While the reason for Teacher Yu's urgent call to duty at the primary school remains unclear, his enthusiasm and quality of leadership seem to have impressed his new colleagues.

In the meantime, China's growing engagement with the international scholarly community that was dominated by Western powers revealed the knowledge gap that has existed between Chinese and Western academic institutions. The Cultural Revolution halted scholarly exploration in the humanities and the social sciences and nearly destroyed their knowledge base. Academic disciplines that were considered undesirable—non-Marxist Western philosophy, sociology, and psychology, to name just a few—basically stopped functioning as fields of inquiry. While their restoration in the 1980s was applauded, those Chinese academics who returned from academic exile found a chasm of understanding so vast that it would require years for them to trek back to the cutting edge of their own fields. The journey was especially difficult for scholars in such disciplines as philosophy, history, and sociology; for, as fields of inquiry that were devoted to exploring phenomena in human society, they had to avoid contradicting the orthodoxies of Communism, the state-sponsored ideology. As Western ideas and practices flow into China, the party-state has exercised vigilance on their effect on the intelligent-sia and higher institutions since maintaining political rectitude has always had priority over cultural pluralism in society. Historically, China had shifted its stance in its encounters with the Western influence, causing it to waver between accommodation and rejection. The approach of the present regime has been cautious and tentative, leaving ample room for fear of encroachment of foreign ideas and values to linger (Yuan 2014).

In philosophy, which is Teacher Yu's own field of study, Chinese academics in the Mainland had, for most of the 1980s, observed from the sidelines the debate on neo-Confucianism that took place in Hong Kong and Taiwan (Cheng and Bunnin 2002), while being uncertain of the political status of the ancient sage who was trenchantly criticized in the early 1970s. With a meager knowledge base, the philosophers sought "safer" undertakings such as reverting to the continuous refine-ment of party orthodoxies or translating texts of Western philosophies. In the more relaxed political atmosphere of the mid-1990s when there was more room for intellectual exploration, neo-Confucianism was put on the agenda of philosophical inquiry (Goldman and Lee 2002: 526). The field of philosophy became more diverse. As Confucian scholars dusted off their old collections, others have ventured into academic fields like postmodernism and cultural studies, which were novel sub-fields at the periphery of Chinese scholarship. The philosophers can now settle into pursuits that run the gamut from speculative to analytical philoso-phies. Interestingly, their Western counterparts have already moved on to explore new ways of doing philosophy. In the field of educational studies, for instance, philosophers are experimenting with ways to absorb empiri-cal research into philosophical inquiry (for example, Hansen et al. 2015; Wilson and Santoro 2015).

Whatever their fields of study, Chinese scholars have shared a com-pulsion to worry about their country (*youhuan yishi*). It is a conscious-ness to shoulder the responsibility of solving the nation's problems. This consciousness, which has been embraced by Chinese intellectu-als since the nineteenth century, has affected the worldview of the aca-demics as well as the ways in which they have pursued their scholarship and framed their inquiry. The academics' endeavors, from initiating a research project to taking up an official appointment, are often justified by the belief that they would somehow solve China's problems. Perhaps it was because of this mental burden that the inquiry of Chinese scholars, particularly those in the humanities and social sciences with a manifest tendency to begin and end with China's problems, seldom ventured into the mainstream of the scholarly world. An example of this tendency is the work by scholars in critical theories and postmodernism, who rarely received attention in the mainstream of Western scholarship. For those Chinese scholars who have pursued graduate study abroad, there is also a problem of epistemological transference. As one observer has noted, they "cherry-pick from the theories and models on offer in graduate programs around the world to address Chinese problems. Their writings are not only mostly in Chinese but nearly always cast in the rhetoric or discourse of contemporary sinophone academic and policy concerns" (Cheek 2015: 287).

Teacher Yu seldom used "solving China's problems" as a justification for his action or a reason behind his decisions. But such consciousness is clearly discernible in his thought and deeds. To a certain extent, the decision to devote his doctoral study on postmodernism was made for him by his supervisor who thought that the postmodernist conditions would become a problem in Chinese society and therefore was worth investigating. Moreover, Teacher Yu's continual interest in postmodernism has not engaged him in a sustainable dialogue with overseas scholars in the field; rather, he has chosen to use postmodernism as a perspective to examine China's "modernity crisis" (Yu 2005). In our discussion on important educational issues, solving China's problems formed the basis of his arguments. For example, his advocacy for an authentic education that would enhance the natural attributes of the child appears to be an educator's reaction against the dominance of examinations over China's education system. The closer relationship that he recommends for his school and his students' parents is a way of ensuring that his brand of authentic education could gain the support of the most important stakeholders. Furthermore, the widespread borrowing of Western educational methods in certain schools and institutions has led him to believe, like the reformers of the past, that there should be a clear demarcation of roles between Chinese and Western knowledge in the nation's development, with the latter being used only to inform practice. His concern over the contrariety between Chinese and Western values stems from a desire to reconcile the differences between the two for the nation's progress, even if the integration of opposing values seems improbable.

There is a substantial difference between the concerns of Teacher Yu and those of his predecessors, for he belongs to a generation of intellectuals that worry less about China's survival and more about its achievement. Instead of viewing education as an instrument of "national salvation" like the intellectuals of the May Fourth era, Teacher Yu sees education as an avenue for China to attain greatness. With rapid economic growth, political stability, and rise in international status, Teacher Yu talks about China's educational problems with "Chinese greatness" on his mind. Indeed, "Chinese Aura" provides a convenient point of reference for his ideas and actions.

FORGING IDENTITY AMID CHANGING ROLES

Teacher Yu was assigned to a variety positions within the university that required a range of knowledge and skills. The regular changes in positions, prompted by the range of appointments, have made his identity-building efforts more complicated. The questions of "Who am I?" and "What am I doing?" can only be addressed rather than answered.

By his willingness and efforts in accepting each appointment, and having demonstrated his competence in different capacities, he has distinguished himself, among certain institutional circles, as a troubleshooter who has helped the university tackle thorny administrative problems. Because of the multiple administrative appointments, Teacher Yu was probably identified more as a university official than as a scholar-teacher. Being in the university administration is advantageous to career development, if one wishes to be identified as a leading member of cadre. This is because an administrative position affords the power to control resources and the opportunity to demonstrate one's ability while serving the university leaders directly. The dual administrative system in Chinese institutions where Party functionaries coexist with academics in the management of academic units such as faculty, departments, and research institutes means that the boundaries between political work and academic work can be blurred by concurrent appointments. When the administration is slack in maintaining discipline, this system may allow certain individuals to cross functional boundaries. In Chinese universities, it was not uncommon for Party functionaries to pick up academic titles, such as "professor" and "researcher," even when such exploitative practice was loathed. Of course, in the dual administrative/academic system, there are surely academics who serve Party functions concurrently, yet most of them perform certain academic duties and many would identify themselves as faculty members.

During our conversations, Teacher Yu never professed any reluctance to work for the Party or the university administration, but he obviously savored the accomplishments of his academic endeavors. He chose to pursue the academic route after he became an experienced instructor in political education and a high-level Party functionary in the Faculty of Education. His enrollment in the faculty's doctoral program was an attempt to establish himself as a "true" scholar with an identifiable specialization. At the turn of the century, it was fashionable among government officials and university administrators with good connections to acquire doctorates from higher institutions without the necessary exertion of effort. In a sense, this kind of acquisition by well-placed officials can be seen as transference of prestige from academia to official. Teacher Yu's choice to pursue doctoral study in philosophy of education under a mentor who was known for his scholarly rigor and attention to quality should signify his intention of becoming a "true" scholar. After completing his doctoral study, he continued to establish his scholarly presence with a steady flow of books and journal articles and through participation in academic associations and conferences. Now, he is identified as a noteworthy scholar in the field of philosophy of education in China with a specialization in postmodernism, and by his appointment as the dean of education, Teacher Yu has completed the transition from the political track to the academic track and created a new scholarly identity in the process (Interview 2, 2014: 15).

In playing different roles in the university structure, Teacher Yu's efforts to forge new identities were driven by demands that were embedded in those positions at the time. As a teacher of political education in the university, he had to demonstrate his political rectitude through words and deeds. Even when his students had to undergo draconian measures, such as early morning drills, he had to wait for an opportunity for change in the chain of administrative command, to modify the unreasonable requirements. As a teacher of philosophy of education, his work was driven by reason and curiosity, but his circumspect scholarly pursuit has had to tread the ideological fine line between conformity and transgression. As an educational entrepreneur, he had to balance the interests of students in mass distance learning against the lures of profit-making, and to ensure that the quality of his programs could meet the required standard. The deanship in the Faculty of Education challenged him to cast his vision far and wide for exemplars of excellence and inspiration for change when higher education was in a constant state of competition and experimentation. The headship at the university's primary school afforded him an opportunity to apply his educational ideas to the reality of teaching and learning where traditional and innovative educational practices are locked in a continuous contest.

Teacher Yu's identity-building endeavor can be viewed in two phases. The first phase consists of his work as a student counselor and Party functionary, which spanned over a decade when he devoted his time to being a "king of children," an experienced political teacher, and a budding scholar. The second phase, however, is much less clear and embodies the irony of career advancement in the face of academic diligence. This is because, in recent years, he had barely time to make a mark in one post before being uprooted and transplanted in another substantially different one.

A more general categorization of Teacher Yu's identity is that he is an intellectual and an educator, but these identities, as well as the contexts from which they derive their meaning, have gone through such metamorphosis that they are difficult to recognize through the lens of Chinese Aura. As an intellectual with professional involvement in both schooling and higher education, Teacher Yu is mindful of his obligations in cultivating a balanced worldview that can inform the stakeholders in schooling and higher education. However, the mission of today's schools and universities has transcended the legacy of "national salvation," a notion that was widely shared by past generations of Chinese intellectuals. Instead, an aspiration to greatness has emerged from decades of stability and prosperity that have been translated into a vision of excellence and equality that the schools and universities are supposed to help fulfill. At the same time, the voice of the intelligentsia has become more diffuse as there is a discernible withdrawal of intellectuals from the public sphere (Cheek 2015: 281). The intellectuals have now taken on new identities, as specialists in differentiated fields (writers, artists, and scientists), or as professional experts (educationists, lawyers, and architects), or as learned persons holding occupational titles (professors, researchers, lecturers, and specialized teachers). While such differentiation of identities places emphasis on specialized knowledge and skills, it also causes the intellectuals to become more aloof from the public discourse. Increasingly, if one wants to get something done, one has to go through the officials, who are widely considered as the legitimate arbiters in Chinese public affairs. Reliance on state power to get things done is a prevalent belief in schools, universities, and society today.

Like his fellow citizens, Teacher Yu shares this belief in official power. He was willing to get the party-state involved in initiatives that would benefit his faculty or school, like working with the city government to establish a research unit for basic education when he was serving as dean of education at the university. As an educator, Teacher Yu sees no paradox in acting as a change agent in education and a stalwart of cultural preservation. From our conversations, his major concerns are issues generated from the interaction of tradition and modernity and from the contrariety of indigenous and foreign values, knowledge, and practice. He cited critical events that helped to illustrate his views on these issues, and borrowed profound ideas from the Confucian classics to elucidate the possible integration of the change forces. Yet, he has been aware of the limitations of his scholarship and the fading relevance of philosophy to the realities of the schools and universities. "You can't expect to change the reality with an essay," he once pointed out the limitation of philosophical discourse in the face of China's educational dilemmas (Interview 3, 2014: 13). He now works in a primary school and considers his work there as "real education that is alive, education with flesh and blood" (Yu and Qin 2009: 28).

It is from the vantage point of a school principal that Teacher Yu may experience the problem of "doing education" while retaining the healthy skepticism of a philosopher toward certain "creative solutions" to China's educational problems, such as the "flipped classroom" approach for teaching and learning in schools and the formation of professional learning communities for teachers. The effectiveness of these "solutions" in the Chinese context awaits evidence from empirical research. In "doing education," he may also have to demonstrate the efficacy of what he proposes as school policies as well as to maintain a delicate balance between the aspirations of his students and their parents, on the one hand, and his own beliefs in the aims of "good education," on the other hand. To achieve this goal, he may even have to counsel himself against the temptation of borrowing from "advanced experiences" of the West and to caution his staff about the likely repercussions of implementing well-intentioned but ill-conceived reform.

As an educator and an intellectual, Teacher Yu has had to contend with the three traditions that were discussed earlier. First, in the role of a university teacher serving in different academic and administrative positions, he has learned from the first tradition, the millennia-old cultural tradition, to have faith in the stabilizing effects of the social structure and in the power of policies to change things for the better. He recognizes the fallacies of an examination-oriented pedagogy, but thinks that the examinations perpetuate an effective system of selection that ensures a certain degree of fairness for university admission and social mobility. Moreover, while being critical of certain ineffectual reform measures, he believes that the timely implementation of good policies can effect desirable changes. China's cultural tradition embodies the wisdom and good practices that can be tapped and revived for solving contemporary problems.

Second, as a scholar specializing in philosophy of education, he inherited the critical and participatory spirit of the second tradition which stemmed from the May Fourth Movement. He is critical of the singularity in thinking and the uniformity in approach that have characterized educational ideas and practices in his country, but he also looks upon the emerging cultural pluralism with hope and the educational changes with optimism. He is receptive to the knowledge and ideas imported from the West, and thinks that they present a welcomed challenge to the orthodoxies that have prevailed in the education system. He assumes that through a process of modification, transformation, and creation, some of the imported ideas can be modified to suit the reality of Chinese education.

Finally, as a witness of history and with the experience as a "political worker" in higher education, he observed the violations and abhorrent practices that were bred by the third tradition, the revolutionary tradition that was based on political fervor. From those episodes, he tried to understand the darker side of human nature, as in the "banality of evil," and to recognize the essentiality of tolerance in educational and social settings. He believes that it is from tolerance and leniency that grows the enactment of human compassion genuine and consequential.

OFFICIALISM AND THE BASIS OF DOCILITY

The traditional career pattern of Chinese academics is one job under one employer until retirement. The nature of their jobs was mainly academic, and even when they took up concurrent appointments in the same institution, their main duties were still related to scholarly pursuits. Teacher Yu's experiences reflect a new pattern in career development: When people are deemed to possess the required knowledge and skills for certain jobs, they can be moved to different positions within the organizational structure of the university on short notice. What are the factors that have made the changes in Teacher Yu's career possible? And why was he willing to make the kind of career shifts that required him to develop new mind-sets and knowledge?

On his career shifts, Teacher Yu recalls that the appointments were "decided by the leaders" and he "obeyed." If the assignments to different positions are considered as "promotions," then he was "being promoted" by "external forces" (Interview 5, 2016: 4). He says:

> My advancement can be considered as 'being passive promotion.... The few [career] shifts that occurred recently were the results of external effects. For example, from the assignment to deputy director of student affairs, to being the Party secretary of the Faculty of Education, and to various positions later, like being the principal of the affiliated primary school, they were all decided by the leaders. I basically obeyed. Only once did I disobey. This was when they wanted to assign me to head up a publishing conglomerate. I was quite firm and did not agree. I told them I couldn't do it. The matter was dropped and was never mentioned again. (Ibid.)

And, as if to find a reason for his unwavering loyalty, Teacher Yu adds: "I have a pretty strong organization mindset" (Ibid.: 7).

Regarding the "strong organization mindset" that Teacher Yu believes he possesses, there are two cultural strands in Chinese organizations that may help to explain his acceptance of frequent positional transfers. The first cultural strand is related to "officialism," a historical phenomenon that delineates the reach of official power. The second cultural strand is composed of the intricate relationships between the holders of power and those who benefit from their actions in groups that share certain commonalities. These commonalities are mostly social and political, such as ancestral lineage, educational background, associational identity, and political affiliation. In an institutional setting, both of these strands may have an effect on the decisions of individuals who are obliged to consider their relations with individuals and groups with power. When they consider that consent or acquiescence can best serve their interests, docility becomes the basis of their actions.

In traditional China, "officialism" found its expression in official power and authority that dominated the society and caused authority relations to become the most important social relations (Yu 2014). A system of "officialism" operates on the logic of hierarchical power and authority. Those in authority attempted to secure their privileged positions by setting up moral codes and social rules, recruiting people with merits, ranking these people in an elaborated system of authority status and power, and rewarding them in accordance with their official status (Ibid.: 2, 4–5). The "people with merits" were educated persons who became the officials of old cultural tradition. They are the predecessors of modern day cadres who also work in elaborated systems of status and power that are still found in Party and government bureaus and state enterprises. On the surface, the modern Chinese universities are a far cry from such a system of management because they, as institutions of higher learning, are supposedly run by scholars whose authority is based on knowledge and not on power. However, the operation of Chinese universities suggests that officialism is alive and well there—the dual system of administration that favors the Party's political power and authority; the exaggerated status of administrative offices and those in leadership positions; the clear hierarchy for the Party functionaries and for academics; the deference accorded to state officials; and the equivalence drawn between academic ranks and official ranks used in government. These practices have emerged from the mind-set of officialdom and are instilled in the mental models of the university community.

Teacher Yu has maintained a long and enduring relationship with his university. Like many academics of his generation, he has spent his whole working life in the same institution which educated him when he was young, employed him when he needed a job, and provided him with job security for over three decades. It will continue to pay him a salary after he retires. The university provides the foundation of his academic, professional, and associational identities, as well as memories that are imbedded in his personal history. But what kind of an institution is the university? Is it government? Or is it a cousin of the state enterprise?[2] Are the leaders of universities academics or members of cadres? Teacher Yu learned very early in his career that one could not join a cadre without being accepted as a "person of merit" that deserves to be in a position of responsibility. His long service as a student counselor notwithstanding, Teacher Yu was not considered one of a cadre until he was given an official position in student affairs. With that appointment, he was no longer just an ordinary "political worker" but one with real responsibilities. One such responsibility is to accept and to live by the rules of officialdom as it is expressed in Chinese academia. It means to obey the "decisions of the organization." Here, the "organization" becomes an expression of official power and authority ensconced in its own abstraction. The "organization" defies definition, for it is meant to remain fluid and nebulous.

Depending on the circumstances, the "organization" may be a committee of decision-makers, or a few, or simply just one person who wants to get things done.

Teacher Yu had no problem understanding the university as an "organization" or relating to those significant persons who constitute the "organization" for him. It was because of the "organization" and the significant persons in it that Teacher Yu obeyed the assignments to new positions in relatively short time spans. In retrospect, he attributes his career advancement partially to the docility that he has displayed through the years. He says:

> [I have] basically obeyed the organization's assignments. There were other teachers and colleagues who were also suitable for these positions. But some of them might not have obeyed [the assignments], or firmly disobeyed. There were [assignments to] positions to which I objected. But after being guided and persuaded by the organization, I basically obeyed. (Interview 5, 2016: 7)

It has been said that people working in an institutional environment tend to comply because of a variety of reasons: fear of reprisal, maximization of benefits, sense of moral duty, reflexive response to uncertainty, or absence of an alternative way of acting (Lo and Ye 2017). In that kind of environment, people can reproduce, sustain, and reform the system that they work in when opportunities avail themselves. They can either work as preservers of institutional norms and values or as human agents to change the system for the better. From his account of his experiences, Teacher Yu seems to have wanted to do both.

The persons in the organization who "guided" and "persuaded" Teacher Yu must have been important to him. Throughout his tenure at the university, he has nurtured relationships with persons who have earned his trust, respect, and allegiance. From his mentors and teachers to his supervisors and colleagues, there are persons whom he looks up to, wants to emulate, or is beholden to. These persons are those who have enlightened and guided him through different stages of his career. The teachers who reminded him of the essentiality of scholarly pursuits in the university environment, those who taught him writing and lecturing skills, and those who set examples for his behavior and action are all remembered with fondness and respect (Interview 5, 2016: 3). The university leaders who identified his strengths and assigned him to positions that facilitated the demonstration of his diverse capabilities are acknowledged gratefully as the "leadership" or "organization." For Teacher Yu, it is the attention and deeds of all of the above parties that have given him the opportunities to excel. While "remembering the spring that bestows the drinking water," he has been mindful of reciprocating the bestowed favors.

The relationships between Teacher Yu and his mentors and sponsors represent a constant balancing of sponsorship and protection, on the one hand, and reciprocation and requital, on the other hand. In certain academic discussions (Yang 1987; Lo 1991), they refer to the relationships between power holders, such as state officials, university leaders, and thesis supervisors, and those who benefit from their deliberate actions, such as ordinary citizens, employees, junior faculty, and students. The sponsorship of power holders may take various forms of approval, such as promotion, assignment to desirable jobs, or support of bids to win competition. The beneficiaries' ways of reciprocation are equally varied, but their compliance and docility can be assumed.

The beneficiary's way of reciprocation normally reflects an appreciation of the sponsor's character and deeds. Teacher Yu's appreciation of his sponsors at work has found different ways of expression as well. The most illustrative of the sponsorship–reciprocation relationship is his relationship with Prof. Wang, his doctoral supervisor. Teacher Yu was obviously grateful for Wang's guidance and approval. He describes in detail the arduous process that Prof. Wang had guided him in identifying a research problem for his doctoral thesis and the time that his supervisor had taken to examine the completed work. He recalls with pride the exact of wording of the preface that Wang has written for his book. Teacher Yu appreciates his supervisor's intellectual prowess and scholarly rigor, and he laments his sufferings when Wang was severely criticized for standing up for his own beliefs. In requital, he embarked on something that he knew his late supervisor would appreciate, and that was to launch a scholarly project that is based on Wang's personal history. In a sense, the project takes Teacher Yu's reciprocation to a higher level of appreciation, for, hidden in the scripts and cameras for field research was a yearning for deeper understanding of a beloved mentor.

Teacher Yu's story may not tell us exactly where Chinese education is situated today, but it helps us measure the distance that it has traveled and illuminates the route that it has been inching along. It shows that the ladder of success in Chinese universities can bifurcate into career pathways that require the docility of their professors who will modify their career plans to suit institutional needs. The actions of those who comply with the leaders' directives signify their readiness to sacrifice self-interests for the good of the university. Rewards and sanctions will be distributed in accordance with the perceived effects of their docility.

* * * * * * * * * * * * * * * * *

Afterword: The Principal at His School

It is getting too late for Teacher Yu, the new school principal, to wait for the visitors who are supposed to have arrived half an hour ago. He has to say goodbye to his students, who are queued up in neat lines for a final head count by chaperoning teachers, before they are released to waiting caretakers outside the school gate. The principal is relaxed, mingling with his charges, and chatting with those who want his attention. The simple exercise marks the end of a day at one of the city's most prestigious primary schools.

Teacher Yu's school is situated near the university, but is hidden from view by an ever expanding wall of surrounding buildings. The school has weathered many changes through the years, but its stature never waned. It is frequented by visitors of all kinds: well-connected individuals who seek enrollment for their offspring; admiring practitioners who want to borrow "best practices" from a top school; and city officials who want to show off the school's achievements before their counterparts from other cities and provinces. The school's staff is used to having visitors. So are its students, who greet visitors properly.

Today, the visitors are academics with an interest in the implementation of the school's curriculum, particularly in the teaching and learning of language and culture. When they finally arrive, Teacher Yu had already chosen a spot for a group photo, with the astro-turfed athletic field as a background. A photographer is on hand to record the visit, and an assistant principal in charge of curriculum and teaching matters will serve as a guide for a tour of the school.

Teacher Yu accompanies the visitors on the tour, highlighting special features of the school's facilities for language and art education, and showing student projects in Chinese calligraphy and ink painting to the visitors. But he is at his proudest when the visitors are taken to a spacious conference room that is paneled by half-empty bookcases. There is a group of teachers sitting at a large table, waiting for the seminar to begin. Teacher Yu points out that the conference room was converted from the principal's office and is now being used for study group meetings and seminars. He gestures to the bookcases and promises that they will be filled with books when he moves his collection from the university. "So that we can all read them and discuss them," he says proudly.

The seminar that follows is focused on curriculum planning and evaluation of teaching, but Teacher Yu would occasionally interject his ideas on how teaching and learning can be done authentically, by using the developmental stages of the child as a yardstick of appropriateness. The teachers nod in agreement. While some of them are still trying to comprehend the meaning of the principal's assertions, no one asks a question. The seminar goes on smoothly. Undoubtedly, the principal has a few ideas for the future development of the school. He urges his staff to study to become learned educators for the benefit of the children. He also mentions the importance of working with the parents. The seminar ends with a summary of views being expressed, mostly regarding those voiced by the principal and the visitors.

At the school gate, the visitors ask Teacher Yu where he conducts his business, now that the principal's office has been converted into a conference room. "I move around a lot in the school," he replies, "but if I need a rest, I have a small office in the auxiliary building." He has clearly made the transition from being a university scholar *cum* administrator to being a school principal. In his new role, he brings optimism and a fresh perspective on being a teacher and an educator. He is also trying to change the organizational culture of the school and to forge a closer relationship with the parents.

If there is any regret about his changing work situation, Teacher Yu has not shown it. Perhaps having lived with change throughout his life, the recent transfer is only one of many changes in his career, an episode that can draw him closer to doing education rather than thinking and writing about it.

NOTES

1. This phenomenon is especially apparent in the fields of the social sciences and education. As the Chinese mode of presentation differs considerably from those approaches and styles that are adapted by English-speaking journals, the Western format is cynically termed the "foreign eight-legged essay" in reference to the required format of the Imperial Examinations of old.

2. A possible answer to this question is that both the university and the state enterprise can be categorized as "work-units" ("*danwei*") which as organizations offered not only employment for their workers but also enveloped their lives with provisions that ranged from housing and meals to health benefits and schooling for children of employees. The "work-units" operated on their own paternalistic logic of taking care of their own in the organization. Continual pressure on the "work-units" to alter their costly and burdensome style of operation has brought the custom closer to extinction. But from the expectations of people who have provided long years of service at the universities and state enterprises, the mental habits of "work-units" are very much alive.

References

[CCCPC] Zhonggong zhongyang [Central Committee of the Communist Party of China]. (1985). *Zhonggong zhongyang huanyu tizhi gaige de jueding* [Decision on the reform of the educational system]. Retrieved from www.moe.gov.cn on April 24, 2017.

Cheek, T. (2015). *The intellectual in Modern Chinese history*. Cambridge: Cambridge University Press.

Chen, T. H. E. (1974). *The Maoist educational revolution*. New York: Praeger.

Cheng, C. Y., & Bunnin, N. (Eds.). (2002). *Contemporary Chinese philosophy*. Oxford: Blackwell.

Goldman, M., & Lee, L. O. F. (Eds.). (2002). *An intellectual history of Modern China*. New York: Cambridge University Press.

Hansen, D. T., Wozniak, J. T., & Diego, A. C. G. (2015). Fusing philosophy and fieldwork in a study of being a person in the world: An interim commentary. *Studies in Philosophy and Education, 34*(2), 159–170. doi:10.1007/s11217-014-9410-y.

Hu, C. T. (Ed.). (1974). *Chinese education under communism*. New York: Teachers College Press.

Lo, L. N. K. (1991). State patronage of intellectuals in Chinese higher education. *Comparative Education Review, 35*(4), 690–720.

Lo, L. N. K., & Ye, J. (2017, Forthcoming). The historical context of the role and status of scholars and teachers in traditional China. In X. D. Zhu, A. L. Goodwin, & H. J. Zhang (Eds.), *Quality of teacher education and learning: Theory and practice*. Singapore: Springer.

Wilson, T. S., & Santoro, D. A. (2015). Philosophy pursued through empirical research: Introduction to the special issue. *Studies in Philosophy and Education, 34*(2), 115–124. doi:10.1007/s11217-015-9460-9.

Yang, L. S. (1987). *Zhongguo wenhua zhong bào, bǎo, bāo zhi yiyi [The meaning of bào, bǎo, bāo in Chinese culture]*. Hong Kong: Chinese University Press.

Yu, W. (2005). Jiaoyuguan de xiandaixing weiji yu xinlujing chutan [Modernity crisis of educational perspectives and research on the new route]. *Jiaoyu Yanjiu* [*Educational Research*], *3*, 51–57.

Yu, W., & Y. Y. Qin. (2009). Bentu wenti yishi yu jiaoyu lilun bentuhua [Local issue awareness and the localization of educational theory]. *Jiaoyu Yanjiu* [*Educational Research*], *6*, 27–31.

Yu, K. P. (2014). An essay on officialism (Guanben Zhuyi): A political analysis of Chinese Traditional Society. *Journal of Chinese Political Science, 19*(3), 235–247. doi:10.1007/s11366-014-9297-z.

Yuan, G. R. (2014). Shenhua jiaoyu lingyu zonghe gaige, jiakuai tuijin jiaoyu zhili tizhi he zhili nengli xiandaihua—zai 2014 quanguo jiaoyu gongzuo hui-yishang de jianghua [Deepen comprehensive reform in the education sector, accelerate the modernization of the educational governance system and governance ability—Speech at the 2014 National Education Work Conference]. Author.

BIBLIOGRAPHY

Pinar, W. F., Reynolds, W. M., Slattery, P., & Taubman, P. M. (1995). *Understanding curriculum: An introduction to the study of historical and contemporary curriculum discourses* (5th ed.). New York: Peter Lang.

© The Editor(s) (if applicable) and The Author(s) 2018   117
F. Wang and L.N.K. Lo, *Navigating Educational Change in China*,
Curriculum Studies Worldwide, DOI 10.1007/978-3-319-63615-3

INDEX

© The Editor(s) (if applicable) and The Author(s) 2018   119
F. Wang and L.N. Lo, *Navigating Educational Change in China*,
Curriculum Studies Worldwide, DOI 10.1007/978-3-319-63615-3

CPSIA information can be obtained
at www.ICGtesting.com
Printed in the USA
LVOW13*2015160318

570135LV00015B/504/P